frontline history

Germany

1918 – 1945

Andrew Boxer

SERIES EDITOR: DERRICK MURPHY

Published by Collins Educational
An imprint of HarperCollins*Publishers* Ltd
77–85 Fulham Palace Road
Hammersmith
London
W6 8JB

www.**Collins**Education.com
On-line support for schools and colleges

© HarperCollins*Publishers* Ltd 2003
First published 2003

ISBN 0 00 715505 0

Andrew Boxer asserts his moral right to be identified as the author of this work.

British Library Cataloguing in Publication Data.
A catalogue record for this publication is available from the British Library.

Edited by Will Chuter
Design by Sally Boothroyd
Cover design by BarkerHilsdon
Picture research by Celia Dearing
Artwork by Richard Morris
Production by Sarah Robinson
Index compiled by Julie Rimington
Printed and bound by Printing Express Ltd, Hong Kong

Contents

Using your factual knowledge of Germany between 1918 and 1945 effectively is very important to success in this area of GCSE Modern World History. This book is designed to provide the essential information. It contains:

• The important questions asked at GCSE
• Detailed information about key historical events and characters
• Written and visual sources
• Differing historical interpretations about the period you are studying

This Study Skills section is designed to help you do your best at GCSE Modern World History. Many of the skills are developments from what you covered in Key Stage 3 History:

• How to explain and use written sources
• How to evaluate cartoons, photographs, maps and graphs
• How to develop extended writing

When you are studying the individual topics in this book make sure that you refer back to these pages for guidance.

HOW TO EXPLAIN AND USE WRITTEN SOURCES

You may have learnt at Key Stage 3 that there are two types of source: primary and secondary. Primary sources are either produced at the time of the event or produced after the event by a witness of the event. Secondary sources are those written after the event by someone who did not witness the event. Although knowing whether a source is primary or secondary is important, it is more important to explain whether it is **useful** or **reliable**.

What does a source show?
Sometimes you are asked to explain what a source reveals about a particular subject. **Remember: always look at the precise wording of a question.** The question may only ask you to explain certain parts of the source.

EXAMPLE 1 – look at Source 1, p12

Question What does this source reveal about the support for the Nazi Party between 1919 and 1933?
In your answer, you need to identify that it shows the growth of Nazi support from 0% of the vote in 1919 to 45% in 1933. In particular, it shows the great increase from December 1924, when the Nazis

received 3% of the vote, to 1930, when they received 21% of the vote. However, you should avoid simply describing all the information in the source. Several sections are not relevant for this question. These include information about other political parties, such as the KPD and SPD.

How reliable is a source?
A reliable source is one that contains an accurate or objective view of a past event. Because different people see past events from different viewpoints, it is difficult for any source to be completely reliable. **Be careful: both primary sources and secondary sources may be unreliable.**

What makes a source unreliable?
A source may be unreliable because it contains **bias**. This means that the person producing the source may wish to look at a past event from a particular viewpoint. The person might have a **motive** for producing the source in a particular way.

EXAMPLE 2 – look at Source 3, p23

Question How reliable is this source as evidence of the role of the SA in 1921?
Ask yourself these questions:

• *Did the person writing the source have a motive for being biased?*
Yes. 'Volkischer Beobachter' is German for 'People's Observer' It was the newspaper of the Nazi Party. Because the SA ('stormtroopers') were an important part of the Nazi Party, it would obviously mention them in a supportive way.

• *Does the source contain **objective** or **subjective** information?*
Objective information means factual information. Subjective information means someone's opinion. If a source contains a lot of subjective information, it is likely to be **biased**. This source contains both objective and subjective information.
Objective information: "The NSDAP [Nazi Party] has created its own gymnastic and sports section… It will provide protection for the propaganda activity of the leaders."
Subjective information: "This is intended to bind our young people to form an organisation of iron… It will encourage mutual loyalty and cheerful obedience to the leader."

Even though a source may contain a lot of facts (objective information) it may still be unreliable. **You will need to test the information against your own knowledge or other sources.**

Some of the information in the source is true. However, the source doesn't mention that the SA was a uniformed group within the Nazi Party that acted like a private army. It attacked the meetings and members of other political parties..

How useful is a source?

To answer this question correctly you need to think about exactly whom it's useful to. Usually this appears in the question: 'How useful is this source to an historian writing about…?'

To decide how useful a source might be you need to look at its strengths, then list them. Then decide what the source's limitations are – what it doesn't mention – then list them. Once you have done this, look at your lists. Does the source contain more strengths than weaknesses? If so, you could say that the source is quite useful.

EXAMPLE 3 – look at Source 2, p50

Question How useful is this source as evidence that the Nazis brought prosperity to Germany after 1933?

List of strengths
- The photograph was taken during the 1930s when the Nazis were in power.
- Wannsee is a lake on the outskirts of Berlin and there are large numbers of Germans enjoying themselves whilst on holiday.

List of limitations
- The source shows only one lake near Berlin on one day. It may have been the only example of its kind at the time. One photograph of holidaying Germans is not enough to prove that the Nazis actually brought prosperity after 1933.
- Although it shows Germans on holiday, it does not show any concrete expressions of wealth, like cars, or other luxuries.
- By reading the text on p50, you will see that this holiday at Wannsee was part of the Nazi KdF scheme – partly paid for by the Nazis – designed specifically to let poorer Germans enjoy luxuries like holidays and cars. So, it doesn't show that the Nazis brought prosperity, but it does show they implemented schemes to help poorer Germans.

The source contains only a limited amount of information. You need to **test this information against your own knowledge to decide how useful it is**.

HOW TO EVALUATE VISUAL SOURCES

Cartoons, photographs, paintings, graphs, and maps are all different types of visual sources. **As with written sources, you also need to test the usefulness and reliability of visual sources.**

Posters

Posters are usually produced for a particular reason. They tend to serve the purposes of the person who has paid for them to be made. These people have **motives** for presenting the poster in a particular way.

EXAMPLE 4 – look at Source C, p70

Question What does this poster suggest about the relationship between the Nazi Party and German workers in the 1930s?
This poster was produced in the 1930s. It shows a German worker, of the German Workers Front (DAF – *Deutsche Arbeits Front*). The DAF was the Nazi trade union, designed to control workers, and also win their support. The worker is building a wall, which is part of a new factory.

The poster is making a political point, so there is a motive for showing German workers in this way. The person who produced it was a supporter of the Nazis. It shows that German workers of the DAF are helping to rebuild German prosperity by building new factories. The worker looks strong, happy, and determined. It suggests workers of the DAF are very important in Nazi Germany. Using your own knowledge of the period, you will know that the Nazis destroyed the free trade unions movement in May 1933. You will also know that many workers before 1933 voted for the Social Democrats (SPD) and the Communists (KPD). The poster is trying to suggest that workers and the Nazi Government (represented by the swastika) are working together. It aims to win over German workers to the D.A.F and the Nazi Party.

Photographs

'The camera never lies!' This is a commonly used phrase that is not necessarily true. Sometimes a picture does not tell the whole story. Therefore you need to **test** the photograph by providing **corroborative** evidence. This means using your own knowledge or referring to other sources.

EXAMPLE 5 – look at Source 2, p35

Question Does this photograph prove that Hitler and Hindenburg were political allies?
This photograph shows President Hindenburg greeting Hitler after his appointment as Chancellor on January 30, 1933. They are shaking hands, but does this mean they are political allies? From your own knowledge you can state that Hindenburg appointed Hitler as Chancellor, which suggests that he was in favour of the appointment. This would support the idea that the pair were political allies. However, you will also know that Hindenburg disliked Hitler, and did not want to make him Chancellor. Hindenburg was persuaded to appoint Hitler by his advisers, who included the new Vice-Chancellor, Franz von Papen. Therefore, after testing the evidence against your own knowledge, you can say that this photograph does not prove that they were political allies.

Paintings
Paintings are usually produced for a particular reason. More than likely, they show the views of the person who has paid the painter. With every painting, you should test the accuracy of the painter's view. Ask yourself these questions:

• *Did the painter approve or disapprove of the painting's subject?*
• *Is it likely that someone with a political **motive** paid the painter to paint the picture in that way?*
• *If so, what was the motive, and how is it represented in the painting?*

EXAMPLE 6 – look at Source 3, p55

This painting shows three generations of a family in Nazi Germany. You can say from your own knowledge that it is a very idealized picture, in which all members match Nazi models of perfection. The man is shown in his SA uniform – he works, fights, and protects Germany. His wife is holding a child – she protects and runs the family and home. She has three children – Hitler encouraged large families to ensure the future of his regime. The children are all healthy, with blonde hair and fair skin. They represent Hitler's vision of a racially pure Germany. The grandmother adds to the sense of family support and strength across the generations. They all look calm, content, and healthy.

Clearly, the painter had a motive for painting the picture in this way. From your own knowledge, you can say that the artist would have been a member of the Reich Chamber of Culture (see p46). This meant he would have been asked only to produce art that glorified the Nazi regime, or could serve as propaganda. It is hard to tell if the artist approved of his subject or not, since he may have been forced to paint it.

Graphs, maps and statistical data
Graphs, maps and statistical data are sometimes used to help students understand information more easily than providing a written source.

EXAMPLE 7 – look at Source 2, p27

This source shows changes in output in certain areas of the German economy from 1918 to 1939. Statistical data gives you precise information. It also allows you to see **trends** and dramatic changes in a way that a written source might not. But statistical data can have limitations. Although this source shows percentages of the 1913 output, it does not show the change in actual output for each product (e.g. tonnes of coal or steel). So, it is difficult to tell how high German output was in 1913, compared to other countries. It is therefore hard to judge how serious the drops in output actually were for the German economy.

EXAMPLE 8 – look at Source 1, p18

Maps have a similar value. This map shows the territorial losses of Germany as a result of the Treaty of Versailles in 1919. It allows you to see that Germany lost most territory to Poland and France. In the case of territory lost to Poland, the Polish Corridor split Germany in two, and East Prussia became separated.

EXAMPLE 9 – look at Source 2, p20

Diagrams can be very useful in identifying **links** between different historical events. This diagram shows the rapid rise in inflation in Germany during 1923. It allows students to see the spectacular collapse in value of the German currency (mark). It can also be used as a basis for discussion. What caused the rapid rise in prices (inflation)?

HOW TO ANSWER EXTENDED WRITING QUESTIONS

These questions require a detailed factual answer. Knowing the information contained in this book is extremely important. To make sure that you use the information correctly you need to:

• **Make sure you answer the question on the paper.** It's a bad idea to write an answer for a question that is not on the paper just because you have prepared for it!

• **Make a short plan for your intended question.** This should show the order you want to set out the information in your answer. It will also help ensure you don't leave out important information whilst writing your answer.

- **Write in paragraphs.** Each paragraph should contain an important point you wish to make.

- **Remember important dates.** Or try to remember the sequence of events.

- **Use historical terms** (e.g. disarmament, remilitarisation, appeasement, nationalism) **correctly. Also use key words** (e.g. Chancellor, President, Führer) **correctly.**

- **Understand the role of important individuals** (e.g. Hitler, Presidents Ebert and Hindenburg, leading Nazis like Goering, Goebbels and Himmler).

- **Make sure you spell historical words correctly.** You must also try to use good punctuation and grammar. Poor 'SPG' can cost you marks.

- **Try to make links between various paragraphs.** If you are asked to explain why Hitler was able to become Chancellor in January 1933, it is important to link causes. They could be:

Long Term Causes German dislike of the Treaty of Versailles, and the weakness of the Weimar Constitution.

Short Term Causes The economic depression after 1929, and the rise of Nazism in Germany after 1929.

Immediate Cause Hitler's unwillingness to accept any post in the government other than Chancellor, and Papen's persuasion of Hindenburg to appoint Hitler.

Or you could mention causes in order of importance. If you do this, give an explanation for putting them in that order.

- **Write a brief conclusion.** This could just be one sentence at the end. But it is essential because it contains your **judgement**. For example, in the question above, what would you regard as the **most important** reason behind Hitler's appointment as Chancellor in January 1933?

HOW THIS BOOK MATCHES THE EXAM SPECIFICATIONS

Chapters in this book	AQA History B, Paper 2, Option B	Edexcel History A, Paper 2, Section B	OCR History B, Depth Study A
1 THE EARLY YEARS OF WEIMAR GERMANY, 1919-23	9.4 Part 1: Weimar Republic, 1918-1933; 9.4 Part 2: Hitler and the growth of the Nazi Party to 1933	N/A	Key Question 1: Was the Weimar Republic doomed from the start?
2 WEIMAR GERMANY, 1924-33	9.4 Part 1: Weimar Republic, 1918-1933; 9.4 Part 2: Hitler and the growth of the Nazi Party to 1933	B4: Nazi Germany, c1930-1939	Key Question 1: Was the Weimar Republic doomed from the start?; Key Question 2: Why was Hitler able to dominate Germany by 1934?
3 THE NAZI DICTATORSHIP	9.4 Part 3: Establishment of a Nazi dictatorship, 1933-1934; 9.4 Part 4: Nazi rule in Germany, 1934-1939	B4: Nazi Germany, c1930-1939	Key Question 3(a): How effectively did the Nazis control Germany, 1933-45?
4 LIFE IN THE THIRD REICH	9.4 Part 4: Nazi rule in Germany, 1934-1939	B4: Nazi Germany, c1930-1939; B5: The World at War, 1938-1945	Key Question 3(a): How effectively did the Nazis control Germany, 1933-45?; Key Question 3(b): What was it like to live in Nazi Germany?
5 PREPARING FOR WAR	9.4 Part 4: Nazi rule in Germany, 1934-1939	N/A	Key Question 3(b): What was it like to live in Nazi Germany?
6 GERMANY AT WAR	N/A	N/A	Key Question 3(b): What was it like to live in Nazi Germany?

Germany in 1918

THE GERMAN EMPIRE

Germany was a powerful country in 1918, but it was also a new one. Until 1871 the German people lived in several separate, independent states. Between 1864 and 1871, the largest German state, Prussia, fought a series of short wars to bring these states under its control and create a German Empire.

GERMANY'S FEDERAL STRUCTURE

This new Germany, united in 1871, was a federal empire. This meant that each of the 22 states within the empire kept its own government and made its own laws about education, taxes, and citizens' rights and welfare. Four of the states, including Prussia, continued to be ruled by monarchs. Prussia's king was also Kaiser (Emperor) of all Germany.

HOW WAS GERMANY GOVERNED?

Germany had some democratic features. Laws for the whole country could be made only by the parliament (called the Reichstag), elected by all German men (women were given the vote in 1919). But the Kaiser retained enormous power.

He commanded the armed forces, decided Germany's foreign policy and chose and dismissed the prime minister – known as the Chancellor – who ran the central government. He could also summon and dismiss the Reichstag.

KAISER WILHELM II

The Kaiser in 1918 was Wilhelm II. He had reigned since 1888. An accident at birth had left him with a withered left arm, and his self-consciousness about this probably explains his frequently eccentric behaviour. He was determined to resist any reduction in his power. He was so worried about the growing popularity of **socialism** that he even considered using the army to close down the Reichstag.

Kaiser Wilhelm II in 1918.

socialism
movement to make the country fully democratic, with equal rights for everyone

Germany in 1914.

GERMANY AND THE OUTBREAK OF WAR IN 1914

Rivalry with Britain
Wilhelm II was jealous of the power and size of the British Empire and decided to build a navy to rival the Royal Navy. He claimed that it was needed to protect Germany's colonies in Africa and the Far East. The race between the two countries to build newer and better battleships was the principal reason Britain and Germany became enemies.

Tensions in Europe

Germany had one of the largest and best-equipped armies in Europe. This worried the French, who had lost two provinces – Alsace and Lorraine – to Germany in 1871. France's main ally was Russia, which meant that Germany was sandwiched between two enemies. Germany's only firm ally was the crumbling Austria-Hungarian Empire. This was in dispute with Russia over who should control the Balkans, in southeast Europe.

These tensions contributed to the outbreak of the First World War in 1914. Germany, supported by Austria-Hungary, fought a long, costly and destructive war against Britain, Russia and France from 1914 until 1918.

GERMANY'S ECONOMY AND SOCIETY

Natural resources

Germany's war effort was backed by its natural wealth and resources. By 1914, it was producing more steel than Britain and almost as much coal. Germany was also a world leader in a number of new technologies, such as car making, chemicals and electrical engineering. This rapid industrial expansion increased the number of workers living in cities. Many of these voted for the Socialists because they wanted the recognition of trade unions, better wages and more equality in German society.

Class divisions

These demands were resisted by Germany's powerful industrialists and by the traditional ruling class, the landowners (*junkers*). The junkers still dominated society, politics and the military, despite the rise in importance of industry. Half of Germany in 1918 was middle class. Those who lived in cities and large towns as professionals, like doctors, lawyers or journalists, wanted to see Germany develop into a democratic monarchy like Britain. Much of Germany's middle class, however, lived in small towns or villages. They saw themselves as the respectable backbone of German society. They were worried by the changes to their traditional way of life brought by industrialisation.

GERMANY'S POPULATION

Race

The German Empire contained three significant racial minorities. Most of the population of Alsace-Lorraine was French, and there was a Danish minority in the northern state of Schleswig-Holstein. Territories in eastern Prussia had mixed German and Polish populations. The Germans had tried to eliminate the culture of these minority groups by such policies as banning the use of their languages in schools. But this only made the racial minorities dislike German rule even more.

Religion

German citizens were not even united in their religion. Predominantly Christians, two-thirds of Germans were **Protestant** and a third **Roman Catholic**. Many in the Roman Catholic states disliked being part of an empire dominated by Protestants.

Protestants
Christians who do not accept the Pope's authority or the ceremonies and rituals of Catholics

Roman Catholics
Christians who recognise the Pope as the head of their Church

GERMANY'S PROBLEMS IN 1918

The Kaiser had hoped that a swift victory in the First World War would prevent Germany's social, political and racial tensions undermining his rule. But four long years of war against a powerful coalition soon began to take their toll on his position and on the mood of the people.

Questions

1. Draw up two columns. In the first column list the people who wanted to change German society in some way. In the second column list those who did not want change.
   a) Which list is longer?
   b) Which groups exercised most power?
2. In what ways did the Kaiser contribute to the outbreak of the First World War?
3. 'It would have been hard for Germany to win the First World War'. Do you agree with this statement? Explain your answer.

War and defeat

DEATH AND INJURY

The First World War had begun with high hopes of German victory in August 1914, but it soon became unbearable for ordinary Germans. The casualty rate was appalling. Of the 10.7 million men who served in the German army during the war, over 60 per cent became casualties. More than two million German servicemen died and approximately 2.7 million survived with a permanent disability. The war created over 500,000 widows and left more than a million orphans.

THE HOME FRONT

For those left at home during the war, daily existence was a struggle to survive. The absence of so many men, away at the front, placed a huge burden on those that remained, especially German women and young people. By 1917, most German farms were run by women. More jobs became available as war industries expanded and wages rose. However, these benefits were cancelled out by rapidly rising prices, caused by shortages of food and other goods. The average weekly wage in Germany doubled during the war, but prices quadrupled. The British naval blockade of German ports and the shortage of labour meant that food supplies were badly disrupted. Although rationing was introduced in 1915, the ration amounts were repeatedly cut as supplies dwindled. When the potato harvest failed in 1916, Germans were forced to make do with turnips throughout the winter.

SOURCE 1 — Destitute Berliners after the end of the war, 1918.

SOURCE 2	The First World War: average wages and prices in Germany.

Monthly wages of a railway guard	
1914	157 marks
1918	342 marks

Price of a kilogram of butter	
1914	2.6 marks
1918	30 marks

DISCONTENT

In 1917, these pressures produced discontent. In April 300,000 Berlin workers went on strike to protest about a cut in the bread ration. Their example was copied in four other cities. By July, disillusionment with the war had even reached the German parliament (Reichstag), which voted to make peace immediately.

GERMANY'S MILITARY DICTATORS

Unfortunately, power in Germany at this time was in the hands of its military leaders, Hindenburg and Ludendorff, not the Reichstag. They ignored the vote and became even more determined to press on with the war in the hope of securing a German victory. They knew they did not have much time because, in April 1917, the USA, with its vast supplies of manpower and industrial might, had joined the Allies.

THE LUDENDORFF OFFENSIVE

In 1917 there was a revolution in Russia. This took Russian attention away from the war, and Germany was able to clinch victory on its eastern front (the Russian border). Ludendorff decided to launch a massive attack in the west. This, he hoped, would achieve victory over Britain and France before American assistance became decisive. The German attack, launched on March 21, 1918, was initially successful. By the summer the Germans were close to Paris.

German prisoners of war after the Battle of St. Quentin Canal, France, October 1918.

desertion
soldiers leaving the armed forces without permission

But the advance had been achieved at the cost of 800,000 German casualties and prisoners of war. War-weariness and defeatism became widespread, and the number of **desertions** increased rapidly. When the Allies, supported by over one million American troops, counter-attacked in July, they were rapidly successful. By the end of August, the Germans had lost all the gains made earlier in the year and Ludendorff realised that the war was lost.

THE GERMAN SURRENDER

Germany's allies (Austria-Hungary, Bulgaria, and the Ottoman Empire) all suffered shattering defeats in the autumn of 1918. Ludendorff told the Kaiser to appoint a civilian government in place of the current military one. He hoped this might persuade the American President to offer lenient peace terms. Ludendorff himself fled to Sweden wearing a false beard. At the end of October, he ordered his fleet to make a last defiant gesture by attacking the British navy. This provoked mutiny and, within days, the sailors, soldiers and workers of Germany's ports and cities had set up their own councils to govern themselves and their own areas. It looked as though Germany was about to follow Russia into turbulent social and political revolution.

On November 9 the Kaiser was finally persuaded to abdicate, and the leader of the Socialist Party, Friedrich Ebert, was appointed to head the government. Germany was now a republic. Ebert knew that the war was lost and, on November 11, 1918, the German armed forces surrendered.

Source 4

From a letter from Hindenburg to the German Chancellor, October 2, 1918.

'We cannot replace the very heavy losses we have recently suffered. This means there is no longer any prospect of victory. Our enemies are regularly bringing fresh reserves into action. It is imperative to stop fighting to spare the German people further useless sacrifice.'

Questions

1. Study Sources 1 and 2. In what ways do they support each other?
2. Study Source 2. How many kilograms of butter could a German railway guard buy with his monthly wages in 1914? How many could he buy in 1918?
3. List as many reasons as you can for Germany's defeat in 1918. Use information and sources in this section.

Germany's political divisions

When Ebert became Germany's political leader in November 1918 he faced a daunting range of problems. He had to try to negotiate a satisfactory peace treaty with the victorious allies (see p18). The **demobilisation** of approximately six million men and the transformation of Germany's economy to peacetime conditions needed to be rapid to enable ordinary Germans to get back to work and feed themselves. Finally, Ebert had to establish law and order in Germany. This meant creating a new **constitution**. This would not be easy because German society was deeply divided and its political groups were bitterly opposed to one another.

demobilisation
men leaving the armed forces officially, to become civilians

constitution
the set of rules by which a society is governed

WHAT WERE GERMANY'S POLITICAL PARTIES?

The **left-wing** parties wanted to change Germany's traditional social structure and give more power and influence to the workers and peasants. The **right-wing**, conservative parties believed that the old social structure should remain. They fiercely resented Germany's defeat and its subsequent weakness. Some wanted to see the monarchy restored; others believed that only a tough dictator could make Germany strong again. Between these two extremes was the Centre Party.

left-wing
believing that society should be made more equal

right-wing
believing that the country should be strong and that ordinary people should have little or no power

SOURCE 1   Percentage of votes won by each party in four elections during the Weimar Republic.

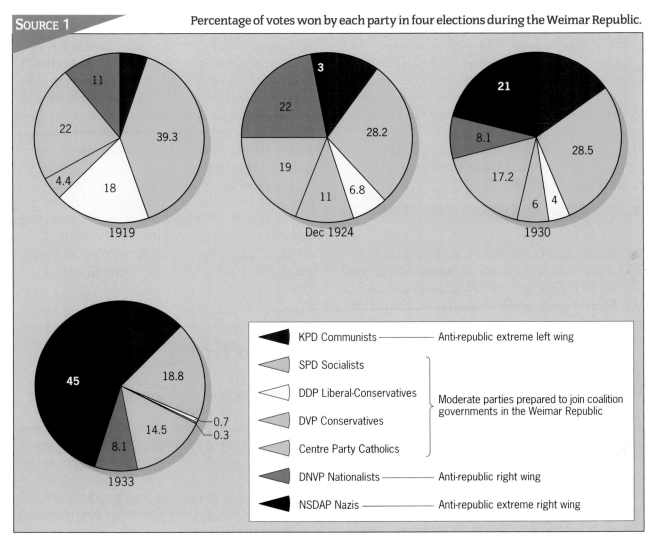

KPD Communists —————— Anti-republic extreme left wing

SPD Socialists

DDP Liberal-Conservatives

DVP Conservatives

Centre Party Catholics

}Moderate parties prepared to join coalition governments in the Weimar Republic

DNVP Nationalists —————— Anti-republic right wing

NSDAP Nazis —————— Anti-republic extreme right wing

THE LEFT-WING PARTIES

The two left-wing parties were the SPD and the KPD. When the Kaiser's government collapsed, they seemed to be strong. But the events of 1919 made them into bitter enemies.

The SPD

(Social Democratic Party of Germany)
Germany's Socialists were the largest party in the Reichstag. They became the main supporters of the new Republic. They had strong links with the trade unions and were supported by the working class, especially the older and skilled workers. They wanted Germany to have a fully democratic constitution.

The KPD

(Communist Party of Germany)
The KPD was formed in December 1918 when some extreme socialists joined Germany's Communists. (These Communists called themselves the Spartacists, in honour of a slave who had led a revolt against the Roman Republic in 73BC). The KPD's support came exclusively from the working class, usually the unskilled, younger workers. They wanted to seize power by force and run Germany as a communist state like Lenin's Russia. This meant breaking up the landed estates, giving the workers control of industry, and reforming the armed forces. Germany's conservatives were divided, and

THE RIGHT-WING PARTIES

supported three different parties. The DDP (German Democratic Party) and the DVP (German People's Party) were supported by businessmen and middle class professionals, such as doctors, lawyers and teachers. The **DNVP** (German National People's Party) attracted nationalists who resented Germany's defeat and disliked the Republic because it seemed to give power to left-wingers. The **NSDAP** – although nonexistent in 1919 – took this nationalism to its extreme.

THE CENTRE PARTY

The **Centre Party** was led and supported by Germany's Roman Catholics, who formed about a third of the population but were mainly to be found in the southern states, especially Bavaria. Unlike the other parties, the Centre Party was supported by all social groups, from the aristocracy to the working class. They became the principal allies of the SPD in supporting the Republic.

These numerous different parties meant that the new Republic was weak from the start. None of them was strong enough to dominate the Republic. The extreme parties of the left and right wanted to overthrow it altogether.

Questions

1. Study Source 1.
   a) When were the Communists strongest?
   b) When were the anti-republican right-wing parties strongest?
2. a) Which parties might be persuaded to support the new Republic?
   b) Which parties wanted to overthrow it?
3. In what ways had Germany's defeat in 1918 made the divisions between Germany's political parties deeper?

The German Revolution of 1919

THE REVOLUTIONARY SITUATION IN GERMANY

A revolutionary group of peasants, workers and soldiers had already seized power in Munich, the capital of Bavaria, two days before the Kaiser's abdication. In Berlin, the power and authority of Friedrich Ebert was being challenged by the workers' and soldiers' council there. All over Germany, similar councils had been set up and claimed power over their local area. The situation was made worse by the demoralised and defeated soldiers of the German army, who wanted to get home as soon as possible. Many simply left the front without waiting for orders, taking their weapons with them. For those who retreated in good order there was a hero's welcome. But the problems of suddenly accommodating, feeding and employing so many ex-soldiers added to the chaos.

> **SOURCE 1** Instruction from a government council in Berlin to Germany's mayors on how to receive returning soldiers.
>
> 'All old posters that stir memories of the war are to be removed from railway stations, which must be cleaned and decorated. Streets leading from the station must be decorated with triumphal arches and garlands. Streets and houses throughout the city must display festive decorations and there is to be festive music everywhere.'

EBERT'S PACT WITH THE ARMY

Ebert and the army commanders were terrified that extreme revolutionaries might seize control of the workers' and soldiers' councils and, inspired by Lenin's success in Russia in November 1917, try to set up a communist dictatorship.

On November 10 Ebert spoke to Ludendorff's replacement, General Groener, about the situation. They agreed that loyal troops would help Ebert crush Germany's Communists. In return, Ebert would prevent the councils from undermining the authority of the officer corps in the Army.

In December delegates from all the workers' and soldiers' councils that had sprung up across Germany assembled for a national congress in Berlin. Ebert was extremely relieved when, on December 19, this congress voted overwhelmingly to hold national elections for a Constituent Assembly. This would be a specialist parliament whose job would be to draw up a democratic constitution for Germany.

WHAT WAS THE SPARTACIST UPRISING?

But this decision annoyed Germany's Communists, who thought that the opportunity for fundamental change was being thrown away. They believed that the proposed Constituent Assembly would simply leave Germany's old power structure in place. During the night of January 5-6, 1919, the Spartacists tried to seize power in Berlin. Ebert and Groener could call on only a few regular troops, so they summoned the Freikorps units to help defeat the Spartacists.

Revolutionary workers and soldiers during the Spartacist Uprising, Berlin, January 1919.

SOURCE 2

WHO WERE THE FREIKORPS?

Since the armistice, many junior officers and NCOs who did not want to be demobilised had formed themselves into unofficial units. These were known as *Freikorps*, or Free Corps, and were usually named after the officer who recruited and led them. Weapons, uniforms and transport were easy to obtain (see Fact File). It did not take the Berlin Freikorps long to defeat the Spartacists and, by January 12, the revolt was over. About 100 Communists and 13 Freikorps men had been killed. The Communist leaders, Rosa Luxemburg and Karl Liebknecht, were arrested and brutally murdered.

FACT FILE
ILLEGAL WEAPONS
In 1920 the German government calculated that 1.8 million rifles, 8,500 machine guns and 400 mine throwers were being held illegally in Germany.

SOURCE 3

THE REVOLUTION IN BAVARIA

There was even more turmoil in Munich. On February 21, Bavaria's revolutionary leader was assassinated by a young monarchist, causing chaos. By April the Berlin government felt strong enough to send troops, supported by Freikorps units, to Munich to crush the revolutionaries there. They did so brutally and, in a reign of terror lasting several weeks, over 1,000 people were killed.

THE IMPORTANCE OF THE GERMAN REVOLUTION

- The hero's welcome given to the returning troops helped to establish the idea that the German army had not been defeated in 1918. Instead, many Germans believed that their army had been 'stabbed in the back' – undermined by left-wing revolutionaries, many of whom were Jews, who had betrayed Germany to the Allies in order to seize power.

- Ebert's decision to use the army, and especially the Freikorps, to suppress the Spartacists and Bavarian revolutionaries poisoned relations between his Socialist Party and the Communists.

- Because Ebert was so afraid of revolution, he did nothing to remove the Kaiser's supporters from positions of power. These judges, army officers, civil servants and senior policemen disliked the new Republic. They supported it only because it was not as bad as communism.

A Hamburg Freikorps recruiting poster. It reads: 'Comrade! Help me against communism... Join the German Protection Squad.'

Questions

1. Study Source 2. How does it help you to understand why the Spartacist Uprising was crushed?
2. How did the events of 1919 make the SPD and KPD into bitter enemies? Explain your answer.
3. How did the new Republic survive the events of 1919? Use information and sources in this section to explain your answer.

The Constitution of the Weimar Republic

On January 19, 1919, elections were held in Germany to select members of a Constituent Assembly, whose job would be to discuss and approve a new constitution for the nation. The Assembly met in the town of Weimar (see map, p8), away from the revolutionary upheaval of Berlin. Early in February, the Assembly elected Ebert as the first President of the new Republic and chose another SPD leader, Philip Scheidemann, to be Chancellor (prime minister). The new Constitution was approved by the Constituent Assembly at the end of July and came into force in the middle of August 1919.

GERMANY'S FEDERAL STRUCTURE

The new Republic, like the Kaiser's empire, was a federal state. This meant that each of the 17 states had its own government and laws controlling such matters as education and policing. The central (federal) government in Berlin controlled foreign policy, defence, taxation and national services like telephones and railways. It could also overrule a state government in certain circumstances, but the regulations about this were not clear. Prussia was easily the largest state, comprising 60 per cent of Germany, while the smallest, Schaumburg-Lippe, covered only 340 square kilometres.

PRESIDENT AND CHANCELLOR

The new system for governing the whole of Germany was highly democratic. The Head of State was the President, who was elected by the people for a term of seven years. In addition to being Commander-in-Chief of the armed forces, the President selected the Chancellor to run the government. He could also dissolve parliament and call for fresh elections. It was expected that he would choose as Chancellor the leader of the party (or group of parties) who had more members of parliament than any other.

THE REICHSTAG

Germany's parliament was called the Reichstag. Its approval was needed for all new laws. It was elected every four years under a system of proportional representation. This meant that the number of seats awarded to each party was fair depending on the number of actual votes it received. Every German aged 20 or over could vote.

SOURCE 1

The Reichstag building in Berlin.

ARTICLE 48

The constitution also guaranteed individual rights, such as freedom of speech (see Fact File). However, under Article 48, the President could declare a state of emergency and allow the Chancellor to suspend these personal freedoms. This article would play a key role in the breakdown of democracy in the early 1930s (see p35).

· · · · · · · **FACT FILE** · · · · · · ·

PERSONAL FREEDOMS GUARANTEED BY THE WEIMAR CONSTITUTION

- Personal liberty is protected by the law
- People's homes cannot be illegally searched
- Letters and correspondence cannot be opened and read
- People can say, write or print what they like, as long as it's legal
- Meetings can occur, providing they are peaceful and unarmed
- People can form societies, clubs and political parties for any legal purpose

proportional representation
a democratic system where a party is given the same percentage of parliamentary seats as the percentage of votes it wins. If a party wins five per cent of the votes, it will receive five per cent of the seats

PRESIDENT
- Head of State
- Elected every seven years by the people
- Chooses/dismisses Chancellor
- Commander-in-Chief of armed forces
- Calls/dismisses Reichstag
- Can grant emergency powers to Chancellor under Article 48

CHANCELLOR
- Head of central (federal) government
- Chosen by President
- Selects cabinet ministers
- His government must resign if Reichstag demands

17 STATE GOVERNMENTS
- Control state education, police force, social welfare, religion
- Answerable to state parliament

REICHSTAG
- National parliament
- Elected every four years by **proportional representation**
- Makes laws for the whole country

17 STATE PARLIAMENTS
- Elected by proportional representation
- Makes laws for the state

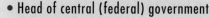

German voters: everyone over the age of 20

CRITICISM OF THE CONSTITUTION

The Weimar Constitution has been criticised by some historians for two reasons.

Proportional representation
This made it difficult for a single party to gain a majority of seats. As a result, every government from 1919 to 1930 was a coalition of two or more parties and each Chancellor remained in power for an average of only nine months. Furthermore, the system allowed small parties, with very little national support, to win seats. However, it was Germany's deep political divisions as much as the Constitution that made its governments unstable.

Article 48
This gave the President and his Chancellor too much power and helped to destroy democracy in the early 1930s. But it is not surprising that this article was included in a constitution drawn up during a year of revolutionary upheaval.

! INVESTIGATE...
What were the strengths and weaknesses of the Weimar Constitution? Go to www.historylearningsite.co.uk.weicons.htm and make a list of strengths and a list of weaknesses.

Questions

1. List the democratic features of the Weimar Constitution. Think about:
   - who could vote, and how often
   - the law-making process
   - how the Chancellor was chosen
   - the ways in which the powers of the government were limited
   - the system of proportional representation
2. Did Germany's federal structure make the country more, or less, democratic? Explain your answer.

The Treaty of Versailles

GERMAN EXPECTATIONS

The Germans had hoped, when they surrendered in 1918, that the subsequent peace treaty would be based on the principles of fairness and justice that President Wilson of the USA had announced in his Fourteen Points in January 1918. Germans were shocked when the victorious Allies first presented their terms to the German government in May 1919. Scheidemann, the Chancellor, wanted to reject them. But, because a British naval blockade would remain in place until the Germans signed, he knew he could not resist, and resigned instead. The new government was forced to accept the terms in June 1919. The Allies had been discussing the terms since January, but there were no German delegates at the signing of this final treaty, in Versailles. To the Germans, the peace terms were nothing more than a *diktat* – a dictated peace.

WHAT WAS IN THE SETTLEMENT?

Territorial losses

Germans were also appalled at the scale of their losses. Germany lost 13 per cent of its territory, including significant industrial areas, such as the coalmining area of the Saar (see Source 1). Nationalist Germans were particularly angry about the loss of land to Poland. This was because some German people – and land they believed to be German territory – were now to be ruled by what they considered to be an inferior Slav race, the Poles.

The 'War Guilt' clause

Article 231 of the Treaty (the clause which blamed Germany and its allies for starting the war) was also resented. Most Germans felt that blame for the war should be shared by all the main powers. They also remembered that Russia had declared war on Germany in 1914, not the other way round.

Reparations

The Allies included Article 231 in the Treaty in order to justify making the Germans pay reparations – compensation for war damage. But to the Germans (and, indeed, to some influential British politicians) it seemed illogical to strip Germany of her wealth (see Fact File), demand high reparations payments and still expect Germany to develop as a successful democracy. The final sum that Germany would have to pay was not settled until 1921.

SOURCE 1

A map showing German land lost in the Treaty of Versailles, 1919.

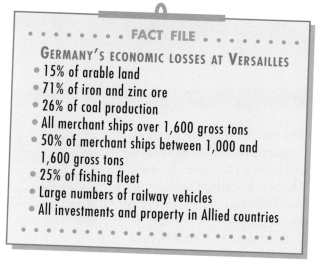

GERMANY'S ECONOMIC LOSSES AT VERSAILLES
- 15% of arable land
- 71% of iron and zinc ore
- 26% of coal production
- All merchant ships over 1,600 gross tons
- 50% of merchant ships between 1,000 and 1,600 gross tons
- 25% of fishing fleet
- Large numbers of railway vehicles
- All investments and property in Allied countries

Disarmament

In addition to losing its navy (which was confiscated by the British) and being forbidden to have an air force, Germany was to be allowed no more than 100,000 soldiers. The Germans were also forbidden to station troops or fortifications in a region approximately 50 kilometres either side of the River Rhine. This Rhineland zone was to be permanently demilitarised.

ALLIED HYPOCRISY

Wilson's Fourteen Points speech about US war aims had referred to a general reduction in armaments, but the peace settlement required only the defeated nations to disarm. Furthermore, Wilson had suggested that people living in colonies ruled by European powers should be consulted about their own future. But Britain and France, who had large colonial empires, were not prepared to do this. Instead, the defeated nations lost their overseas colonies, which were parcelled out among the Allies.

SOURCE 2

VENGEANCE! GERMAN NATION!

Today in the Hall of Mirrors at Versailles, a disgraceful treaty is being signed. Never forget it! Today German honour is being dragged to the grave. Never forget it! There will be vengeance for the shame of 1919!

From the front page of a German nationalist paper.

WHAT WAS THE IMPORTANCE OF THE TREATY OF VERSAILLES?

The Germans were, of course, being hypocritical themselves when they complained about the Treaty. Their own treatment of Russia at the Treaty of Brest-Litovsk in March 1918 was much more savage than Versailles. It is unlikely that, had they defeated France and Britain, they would have offered generous peace terms. Nevertheless, German resentment of the Treaty of Versailles did have important consequences.

German Nationalists

The treaty gave German nationalists cause to hate the Republic because it looked as though Germany's democratic politicians had meekly given in to the Allies.

The 'stab-in-the-back' legend

The treaty strengthened the 'stab-in-the-back' legend. The German army commanders claimed that they had been cheated of victory in 1918 by Jewish left-wing revolutionaries who had betrayed the country in order to seize power. The speed of Germany's collapse between March and November 1918, the absence of fighting on German soil, and the hero's welcome given to returning soldiers all made this story more believable.

Economic problems

The payment of reparations caused economic and political problems for Germany throughout the 1920s and early 1930s.

Questions

1. Study Source 1 and the Fact File. Do the terms imposed on Germany at Versailles justify the anger of the author of Source 2?
2. List the ways in which the Germans thought the Allies were being hypocritical in the terms they imposed on Germany in the Treaty of Versailles.
3. Which terms of the Treaty do you think the Germans hated most? Put them in order and explain your answer.
4. Do you think the Germans were harshly, fairly or leniently treated? Use information and sources in this section to explain your answer.

Reparations and the Ruhr

WHY DID FRANCE AND BELGIUM INVADE THE RUHR?

It was not until April 1921 that the Allies finally agreed the amount to be paid by Germany in reparations. They demanded a sum of £6.6 billion. It was to be paid in money and goods such as coal, timber, chemicals and manufactured products. The Germans protested that they could not afford such a large sum and, in December 1922, asked if they could be allowed to delay payments for two years. The French refused. They thought the Germans were exaggerating their economic difficulties to avoid paying altogether. When the Germans failed to deliver 135,000 metres of telegraph poles, the French government decided to act.

THE INVASION AND PASSIVE RESISTANCE

On January 11, 1923, French and Belgian troops invaded Germany's main industrial area, the Ruhr, to seize for themselves the goods they were owed. This outraged the Germans and united them in hostility to the invaders. The German government ordered workers in the Ruhr to go on strike, but agreed to pay them. This was called 'passive resistance'. The French retaliated by bringing in their own workers, but this only increased the bitterness. To prevent violence, the French authorities sealed off the Ruhr. Germans entering or leaving the Ruhr now had to show their passports to French soldiers and policemen.

SOURCE 1

Occupied by French and Belgian troops, January 1923

GERMANY
R. Ruhr
NETHERLANDS
Cologne
Demilitarised zone
Koblenz
BELGIUM
Mainz
R. Rhine
SAAR
LUXEMBOURG
FRANCE
0   100 km
N

A map of the Ruhr area.

GERMAN INFLATION

The invasion of the Ruhr also triggered the worst period of **inflation** in German history. The value of the German mark in relation to other currencies had been falling since the beginning of the First World War. The shortage of food and other supplies during the war had further increased prices, and Germany's post-war economic difficulties had added to the problems.

inflation
rise in prices due to excess money in circulation or wages rising too rapidly

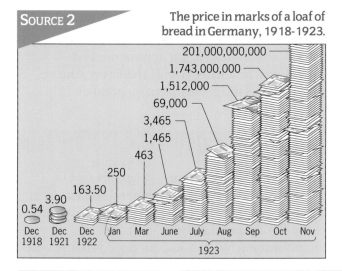

SOURCE 2   The price in marks of a loaf of bread in Germany, 1918-1923.

201,000,000,000
1,743,000,000
1,512,000
69,000
3,465
1,465
463
250
163.50
3.90
0.54

Dec 1918 | Dec 1921 | Dec 1922 | Jan | Mar | June | July | Aug | Sep | Oct | Nov
1923

HYPERINFLATION

The strike by German workers in the Ruhr meant that Germany's main industrial area was not producing anything. As a result, goods were in short supply and shot up in price. This made ordinary Germans demand big pay increases to be able to buy things. The government had to print more notes to keep up with rising prices. This turned inflation into **hyperinflation** and the German currency rapidly became worthless. Many Germans were ruined (see Source 4), although a few managed to exploit the situation and make vast profits (see Source 5). The terrible experiences of 1923 made many ordinary Germans believe that their new democracy had brought them nothing but trouble.

hyperinflation
inflation that is out of control

German children playing with worthless paper money in 1923.

SOURCE 4

A German writer describes a victim of the inflation.

'In the summer of 1923 an old lady asked one of her sons to sell her house. He did so for thousands of millions of marks. The lady decided to keep the money under her mattress and to buy food with it as the need arose. When she died a few months later, nothing was left except a pile of worthless paper banknotes.'

SOURCE 5

The historian Gordon Craig describes the inflation of 1923, in his book *Germany 1866-1945*.

'Lots of people made themselves rich during the inflation. Unscrupulous dealers bought the valuables or family treasures of Germans who were desperate, and then sold them across the border in Holland or Belgium. Black marketeers bought large quantities of food, and sold it for extortionate prices. They spent their profits on lavish meals in expensive restaurants, or took their girlfriends to fashionable nightclubs, paying the bill in dollars or pounds.'

GERMAN 'FULFILMENT' POLICY

By August 1923 it became clear to the German government that the economic chaos could only be ended by fulfilling their obligations. This would mean calling off passive resistance and agreeing to pay reparations. The British and US governments had already signalled that they would help **mediate** a settlement between Germany and France. A new German government, headed by Gustav Stresemann, took office. He stabilised the German economy by issuing a new currency and negotiating the withdrawal of French and Belgian troops.

mediate
to help solve a dispute by acting as a neutral go-between

The Dawes Plan

In 1924 a plan was drawn up by an American banker, Charles Dawes, by which Germany would resume reparations payments to the Allies, the annual amount to be handed over would be reduced, and Germany would receive a large loan to help her economy recover. The Dawes Plan not only ended the crisis of 1923, but enabled the Germans to achieve some prosperity in the 1920s (see p28).

Questions

1. Study Sources 2 and 3. Do they support Source 4? Explain your answer.
2. Some people suffered badly due to the inflation, others survived, and some did well out of it. Place the following six groups of people in order, with those who did worst at the top, and those who did best at the bottom. Use the sources to help you. Explain your answers.
   • Farmers
   • Wage earners (paid weekly)
   • Salary earners (paid monthly)
   • People who had borrowed money
   • Foreign visitors
   • Shopkeepers

The early years of the Nazi Party

THE ORIGINS OF THE NAZI PARTY

The Nazi Party began life as one of a large number of small political groups formed after the First World War. Its original name was the German Workers Party (DAP) and it was founded in 1919 in Munich by a group of railway workers who were shocked by Germany's defeat. They also disliked the left-wing revolutionaries who had seized power in Bavaria at the time. In September 1919 a 30-year-old ex-soldier attended one of their meetings. His name was Adolf Hitler.

WHO WAS ADOLF HITLER?

Hitler was born in 1889 in a small Austrian border town called Braunau, where his father was a customs official. Hitler was not particularly successful at school, although he did enjoy history lessons. Both his parents died while he was still a teenager, and Hitler spent much of his youth in self-indulgent idleness in Vienna. He was rejected by the Vienna art school but believed himself to be much too talented to get an ordinary job.

In 1914 he joined the German army where, for the first time in his life, he felt happy. He enjoyed the comradeship, danger and sense of national purpose that the war gave him. He was twice decorated for bravery, although he does not seem to have shown any special leadership qualities. He was devastated by the news of Germany's surrender and, for the rest of his life, believed the 'stab-in-the-back' legend (see p15). He always referred to the politicians who created and supported the Republic as the 'November Criminals'.

HITLER AND THE DAP

In 1919 Hitler had a job with the Bavarian government that required him to report on the various political protest groups that had sprung up. This was why he attended his first DAP meeting. He was immediately attracted to the party because he knew he would quickly be able to dominate it.

SOURCE 1

Adolf Hitler (right) as a soldier in 1916, during the First World War.

Hitler's impact was immediate. The party's meetings gave him an opportunity to develop his considerable powers as a speaker. He soon became its star attraction, and membership grew rapidly. In February 1920 he changed the party's name to National Socialist German Workers Party (NSDAP), which is where the abbreviation 'Nazi' comes from.

SOURCE 2

A member of the Nazi Party describes his first impression of Hitler as a speaker.

'Hitler was holding the crowd, and me with them, under a hypnotic spell by the sheer force of his conviction. I do not know how to describe the emotions that swept over me as I heard him. I forgot everything but Hitler. Then, glancing around, I saw that his magnetism was holding these thousands as one. Hitler's intense will, the passion of his sincerity, seemed to flow from him into me. I experienced a joy that could only be compared to a religious conversion.'

The 25-Point Programme

He also set out the Party's main aims in the 25-Point Programme. This was a muddled, and slightly contradictory, set of ideas. It shows that the Party was very extreme but also that, in its early days, it was trying to win support mainly from Germany's working class. The 25-Point Programme was a mixture of nationalism, **anti-Semitism** and extreme left-wing notions about the economy.

anti-Semitism
hatred of Jews

Finally, in 1920, Hitler persuaded some wealthy sympathisers to buy control of a newspaper for the Party. It was called *Volkischer Beobachter* – the 'People's Observer'. It enabled the Party to spread its propaganda more widely. Early the following year Hitler made himself the Party's undisputed leader.

THE FORMATION OF THE SA

In 1921 Hitler was able to make use of his army contacts to form the armed section of the party. This was called the *Sturm Abteilung* (SA) – the 'storm section'. The SA were ex-Freikorps men who welcomed the opportunity to stay in uniform and parade behind flags and drums. Their role was to protect Nazi meetings and beat up their opponents. They were organised by Ernst Roehm, a major in the German army who was stationed in Munich (see p43).

SOURCE 3

The *Volkischer Beobachter* announces the creation of the SA, August 1921.

'The NSDAP has created its own gymnastic and sports section. This is intended to bind our young people together to form an organisation of iron, so that its strength will act as a battering ram. It will provide protection for the propaganda activity of the leaders. It will develop in the hearts of our young supporters a tremendous desire for action. It will also encourage mutual loyalty and cheerful obedience to the leader.'

By 1923, the Nazi Party had about 55,000 members, most of whom were also in the SA. Although they had hardly any support outside Bavaria, Hitler believed that the Nazis were powerful enough to overthrow the Republic and seize power.

Questions

1. *Study Source 2. Which words and phrases used by this writer best show the impact Hitler had on him? Explain your answer.*
2. *Study Source 3. Use this source to explain why Roehm was so useful to Hitler in setting up the SA.*
3. *How did Hitler build up the Nazi Party between 1919 and 1923? Explain your answer, using information and sources from this section.*

The threat from the Right: Kapp and Hitler

WHY DISBAND THE FREIKORPS?

In 1919 the Communists had tried to seize power and failed. They had been stopped by the Freikorps, the ex-soldiers who had formed themselves into unofficial fighting units. The government now had no further use for them, and the Allies were demanding that they should be disbanded. The Treaty of Versailles allowed Germany only 100,000 soldiers because this was considered a large enough force to keep order in Germany. Neither the Allies nor the politicians in Berlin wanted gangs of unofficial soldiers roaming around the country.

WHAT WAS THE KAPP PUTSCH?

In March 1920, several Freikorps units decided to seize power rather than be disbanded by a government they despised. They marched on Berlin. The regular army troops refused to stop them. After all, the Freikorps were former comrades and the senior army commanders sympathised with them. Once more, Germany's civilian leaders were forced to flee their capital. This became known as the Kapp Putsch, after the leader of one of the Freikorps units involved. But the Freikorps were not powerful enough to take advantage of their initial success. Berlin's workers went on strike. With government offices, public facilities and transport all at a standstill, the coup collapsed. Like the Communists on the extreme left, Germany's extreme right-wingers were not powerful enough to take power, but they were capable of making the country unstable.

putsch
an attempt to overthrow the government by force. Also called a 'coup'

HITLER'S BEER HALL PUTSCH, 1923

In November 1923 Hitler believed that he could take advantage of the political and economic chaos in Germany to seize power. He knew that the senior politicians in Munich also hated the Republic, so he decided to force them to help him. On November 8 he ordered his SA men to surround the beer hall where the Bavarian leader – Gustav Kahr – was making a speech.

SOURCE 1

Freikorps men with an armoured car and flame thrower in Berlin in 1920.

He then burst in with a small group of armed followers. At pistol point, Kahr and two other Bavarian leaders agreed to support Hitler's coup, which was due to take place the next day. Unfortunately for Hitler, the three politicians slipped away during the night. By the time his march took place the next day, there was little prospect of success. A cordon of police blocked their route from the beer hall to the Munich army barracks where Hitler had planned to gather guns and soldiers. Shots were fired. 14 Nazis and four policemen were killed. Hitler was wounded and fled. Only Ludendorff (see p11), who was to be the figurehead leader, marched through the cordon unchallenged. But, like Hitler, he was soon arrested.

HITLER'S TRIAL

Hitler turned his trial into a propaganda triumph. Charged with treason, he made no apology for his action and claimed that history would prove him right. The judges at his trial sympathised with his views and sentenced him to a mere five years in prison. Ludendorff was acquitted. The publicity surrounding the trial helped to make Hitler a nationally-known figure.

HITLER'S IMPRISONMENT

Hitler served only nine months of his sentence. And he did so in comfortable surroundings. He was allowed regular visitors, and his cell in Landsberg Castle became more like a hotel suite than a prison. He dictated his autobiography, which he called *Mein Kampf* ('My Struggle'). In the book he set out his main political ideas (see Fact File) as well as giving a decidedly misleading account of his life.

Hitler in his cell at Landsberg Castle.

HITLER'S CHANGE IN TACTICS

The most important decision Hitler took while in prison was to abandon the idea of seizing power by force. He realised that he needed to win power legally by gaining votes in the Reichstag. He knew that this would take time, but he also knew that his authority would be greater if he took power legally than if he seized it. However, he was also aware that this new 'legality tactic' would not be popular with everyone in the Nazi Party, especially the SA.

SOURCE 3 — Hitler explains his new tactics in a letter to a friend.

"When I resume active work it will be necessary to pursue a new policy. Instead of working to achieve power by armed conspiracy, we shall have to hold our noses and enter the Reichstag against the Catholic and Communist deputies. Any lawful process is slow, but sooner or later we shall have a majority and after that we shall have Germany."

Questions

1. Study Source 1. How does it help you to understand why the Freikorps were a threat to the Republic?
2. Study Source 2. What does it tell you about Hitler's life in prison?
3. Study Source 3. What reasons does Hitler give for adopting new tactics?
4. How serious was the threat to the Republic posed by the right-wing groups in the years 1919-23? Consider:
   - their ability to get hold of weapons
   - the sympathy they had from those in power
   - their lack of support from the workers
   - their disunity
   - their lack of numbers

   Use information and sources in this section to explain your answer.

The 'Golden Years' of the Weimar Republic

THE WITHDRAWAL OF THE FRENCH AND BELGIANS

Between August and November 1924, the French and Belgian troops withdrew from German soil. Germany resumed paying reparations under the arrangements agreed by the Dawes Plan (see Fact File). With Hitler's Beer Hall Putsch defeated and the threat from the extreme left also eliminated, it looked as though Germany could look forward to some economic and political stability.

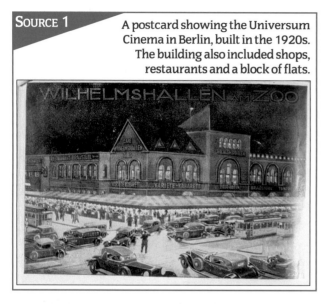

SOURCE 1

A postcard showing the Universum Cinema in Berlin, built in the 1920s. The building also included shops, restaurants and a block of flats.

HOW STABLE WERE GERMAN POLITICS, 1924-1930?

Compared with the early years of the Republic (see the last chapter) and the Depression years of 1930-1933 (see p32), the period between 1924 and 1930 looks very stable. The Reichstag elections of December 1924 strengthened the moderate parties, while the extremists – Nazis and Communists – lost seats. For the next six years Germany was ruled by a series of coalition governments led by the Centre Party and the moderate conservative parties. There were no violent attempts to seize power, and the governments achieved some notable successes, particularly in foreign policy (see p28).

POLITICAL PROBLEMS

However, democracy failed to become firmly established in Germany during this period. The coalition governments never had a strong majority in the Reichstag. This explains why the longest-lasting of them remained in power for only a year. These coalitions might have been stronger had the Socialists (who formed the largest party in the Reichstag) participated. However, they wanted to keep the loyalty of their working class voters, so were reluctant to serve in governments led by conservative ministers.

The death of Ebert

In 1925 President Ebert unexpectedly died. The new President was the 78-year-old Paul von Hindenburg, the Field Marshal who had dominated Germany for much of the First World War. He was one of the men who had created the 'stab-in-the-back' legend (see p15) and he was known to prefer the old monarchy to the new Republic. Furthermore, he was not keen on allowing the Socialist Party into government. However, despite these anti-Republican sympathies, Hindenburg did not use his position to undermine German democracy during this period.

PAUL VON HINDENBURG (1847-1934)

Hindenburg became a war hero when he defeated the Russians at Tannenberg in 1914. From 1916 to 1918 he and Ludendorff ran the country as virtual dictators. He retired when Germany was defeated, but was elected President in 1925. When the political system collapsed in 1930 he used his powers as President to keep a series of conservative Chancellors in power. He reluctantly appointed Hitler Chancellor in 1933, but by then was too old and ill to prevent the Nazis establishing a dictatorship.

ECONOMIC SUCCESS

The Dawes Plan helped to stabilise the German economy. The German banks and federal states also assisted recovery because they offered high interest rates to foreign investors. This brought plenty of money, especially from the USA, into Germany. Industrial production increased steadily during the 1920s (Source 2). German workers were better off in the 1920s because the government increased the amount of money available for unemployment benefit, pensions and sickness insurance.

ECONOMIC PROBLEMS

trade deficit
when a country spends more on its imports than it earns from its exports

But Germany's economic recovery was built on shaky foundations. The foreign loans could be withdrawn at any time. Imports rose faster than exports, meaning that Germany faced a **trade deficit**.

Unemployment remained a problem because the trade unions had succeeded in winning wage increases. This made employers reluctant to take on extra workers. Finally, German farmers did not enjoy much prosperity. In 1927 food prices fell rapidly worldwide. This sharply reduced farmers' income and increased their debts.

. . . . FACT FILE . . . .

THE DAWES PLAN

The Dawes Plan was named after a US banker, Charles Dawes. He headed a special committee to investigate the problem of German reparations. The Plan reduced the amount Germany was required to pay each year. However, the overall amount stayed the same — Germany just had longer to pay it. Full payments would resume in 1929. The Plan came into operation in September 1924.

SOURCE 2

The German economy, 1913-1928: production and trade. From 1919 onwards, figures represent a percentage of 1913's output.

Year	Coal	Oil	Iron	Steel	Exports	Imports
1913	100	100	100	100	100	100
1919	61	31	33	40		
1923	33	42	26	36		
1925	70	65	53	70	66	82
1928	79	76	61	85	87	102

Questions

1. Study Source 1. How does it show that the German economy was recovering in the 1920s?
2. Study Source 2.
   a) Which industry shows the biggest increase in output between 1923 and 1928?
   b) What do the figures for German trade (exports and imports) reveal?

3. How strong was the Weimar Republic in 1928?
   • Draw two columns on a piece of paper, one headed 'Economic success, 1924-1928', the other headed 'Economic difficulties and problems, 1924-1928'. Write down evidence for each under the relevant heading.
   • Do the same for German politics as you did for the economy.
   Use your columns, and information and sources in this section to explain your answer.

Germany and Europe, 1924-29

'FULFILMENT' STARTS

The dramatic events of 1923 convinced politicians in both France and Germany that relations between their two countries would have to improve. The French realised that their invasion of the Ruhr had not been a success. The Germans accepted that they would have to observe the Treaty of Versailles; they hoped that this policy of 'fulfilment' of the Treaty's terms would persuade Britain and France to revise the Treaty in Germany's favour. The man most associated with this policy was Foreign Minister Gustav Stresemann.

GUSTAV STRESEMANN (1878-1929)

Stresemann came from a conservative business background but believed, after 1918, that Germans had to try to make the Republic work. He founded the German People's Party (DVP), which was supported by moderate, conservative middle-class Germans. During his brief chancellorship in 1923, he managed to stabilise the Republic by introducing a new currency. His main achievements were as foreign minister from 1923 until 1929, during which period he successfully negotiated the Dawes and Young Plans, the Locarno Pact and Germany's admission to the League of Nations. His death in 1929 meant that Germany had no outstanding Republican politician to lead the country during the Depression.

THE FOREIGN POLICY OF GUSTAV STRESEMANN

The Dawes Plan and the withdrawal of French and Belgian troops in 1924 were Stresemann's first successes. He quickly realised that he could use Germany's geographical position in the centre of Europe to play the French and British off against the USSR. Neither of the Western powers wanted to see Germany make friends with the USSR, and Stresemann used this to squeeze concessions from them both.

SOURCE 1
From a letter by Gustav Stresemann, September 7, 1925.

'In my opinion there are three great tasks that confront German foreign policy in the immediate future. In the first place, the solution of the reparations question in a way that is tolerable for Germany, and the assurance of peace, which is essential for the recovery of our strength. Secondly, the protection of Germans abroad, those 10 to 12 million who now live in foreign lands. The third great task is the readjustment of our eastern frontiers; the recovery of Danzig, the Polish corridor, and a correction of the frontier in Upper Silesia.'

RELATIONS IMPROVE WITH THE WEST

Locarno
In 1925 Germany, France and Belgium signed the Locarno **Pact**, by which they accepted their mutual frontiers. Britain agreed to ensure that all three countries observed the Pact. Locarno meant that, while Germany appeared to accept the Treaty of Versailles, the French agreed not to repeat their Ruhr invasion. Locarno said nothing about Germany's frontier with Poland. No German would willingly have agreed to accept the boundaries laid down at Versailles, which gave a number of German-speaking areas to Poland.

pact *a treaty or series of treaties*

The League of Nations
The Western Allies also scaled down their military occupation of Germany in 1925. In the following year they withdrew the commission whose job was to ensure the Germans observed the military clauses of the Treaty of Versailles. In 1926 Germany joined the League of Nations and became a permanent member of its Council. This seemed to suggest that relations between Germany and the rest of Europe had entered a new, co-operative era.

SOURCE 2

A modern historian describes the Locarno Pact.

'Locarno was hailed as a great diplomatic triumph. The Foreign Secretaries of Britain, France and Germany were received as national heroes and jointly awarded the Nobel Peace Prize. Their agreement was seen as a milestone on Europe's march to peace and prosperity, and, as a result of the negotiations, Germany joined the League in 1926.'

STRESEMANN'S EASTERN POLICY

Germany had been cautiously friendly towards the USSR since the end of the war. After all, both saw themselves as outcasts in 1919 because neither had been invited to the Versailles Peace Conference. Germany and the USSR had signed a trade agreement in 1922 and, throughout the 1920s, the Soviet Red Army and the German army shared some training facilities and expertise. Both Germany and the USSR disliked Poland and wanted to regain territory from her. But Russia, because of its communism, was unlikely to become a firm ally of a democratic and capitalist country such as Germany.

THE YOUNG PLAN, 1929

Stresemann negotiated another adjustment of Germany's reparations debt in 1929. This was called the Young Plan (see Fact File). Extreme German nationalists, however, did not regard this as a success. They saw it as a shameful betrayal of future generations of Germans because it required Germany to go on paying reparations until 1988.

SOURCE 3

The signing of the Locarno Treaty by Belgium, France and Germany in 1925.

FACT FILE

THE YOUNG PLAN

Named after a US lawyer, Owen Young, who headed another special committee on German reparations. The plan reduced the amount Germany was required to pay overall. The final payment would be made in 1988. The total was now £2.2 billion. The Allies agreed to evacuate the Rhineland in 1930 if Germany accepted the Young Plan. The Germans agreed, but the Young Plan was destroyed by the Depression. The Allies agreed to cancel reparations altogether in 1932. In all, Germany paid about 12 per cent of the original reparations sum demanded, but received in loans a sum equivalent to 20 per cent of the original amount.

Questions

1. Study Source 1. What evidence can you find in this source and the information in this section that Stresemann was a German nationalist?
2. Study Source 2. Why do you think the three foreign secretaries were awarded the Nobel Peace Prize? Give reasons for your answer.
3. Using information and sources in this section, list the ways in which Stresemann's foreign policy contributed to peace in Europe.
4. How far had Stresemann achieved the objectives he outlined in Source 1 by the time of his death in 1929? Explain your answer.

The Nazi Party in the 1920s

THE NSDAP IN 1924

When Hitler was released from prison in December 1924, the Nazi Party had broken up into squabbling factions. This was because Hitler had deliberately appointed an ineffective deputy leader – Alfred Rosenberg – to ensure that it was not successful in his absence. In the Reichstag election of December 1924, the Nazis lost a million votes. The reason for this was that Germans were not interested in voting for an extreme party whilst the country was prosperous and stable.

CREATING THE FÜHRER PARTY

The Party was formally re-founded in February 1925. But, because of his prison sentence, Hitler was banned from speaking in most German states. This meant he had a struggle to reassert his authority. His most serious problem came from a group of Nazis in northern Germany who wanted to commit the Party to a left-wing, socialist programme. In 1926 Hitler persuaded them that the unity of the Party was more important than its beliefs. Absolute loyalty to the leader – the **Führer** – became the Nazis' main idea.

Führer
leader

The SA were also potentially troublesome because they did not like Hitler's new legality tactic (see p25). But they were much too valuable and powerful to be abolished so, in April 1925 he created a personal bodyguard of totally loyal young men, the *Schutzstaffel* (SS), or 'protection squad'.

THE GROWTH OF THE PARTY

The Nazis continued to do badly in elections because Germany was reasonably stable and prosperous in the 1920s. In the 1928 Reichstag elections the Party lost another 100,000 votes and only 12 Nazi deputies (MPs) were elected.

However, the Nazis *were* successful in gradually increasing their membership. During the 1920s, party branches were established all over Germany by fanatical Nazis who regularly toured the country to recruit more members (see Source 3). The country was divided into regions, and a party leader (*gauleiter*) was assigned to each one. By 1929, the Party had about 100,000 members. This meant that it would be well placed to take advantage should Germany's prosperity come to an end.

Hitler at Nuremberg, 1929

SOURCE 1

An early Nazi Party rally in Munich, January 1923.

SOURCE 3 A Nazi account, written in 1937, about the founding of a loyal branch of the Nazi Party in Lower Saxony.

'In the year 1928-29 the Nazi speaker, Jan Blankemeyer, a peasant from a neighbouring district, came and talked to us about Adolf Hitler and his movement. Comrade Blankemeyer then came every two months and in winter even more frequently. After one Blankemeyer meeting eleven people joined the party. Then the SA from another nearby town held a propaganda march, which was followed by a meeting at which our branch was founded, with farmer Hermann Menke as branch leader.'

INVESTIGATE...
What did Hitler and the Nazis do during the Party's 'quiet years' of 1925-1929? Go to www.historyplace.com/worldwar2/riseofhitler/index.htm and write down five events that were important for the Nazi Party in this period.

Questions

1. Study Sources 1 and 2. What do they reveal about the growing strength of the NSDAP in the 1920s?
2. Study Source 3.
   a) How does it help you to understand how the Nazi Party grew during the 1920s? Explain your answer.
   b) How reliable is this source as an account of how the Nazi Party grew in the 1920s?
3. What evidence can you find in this section that the Nazi Party in the 1920s was not as united as Hitler would have liked?

The impact of the Depression

PROBLEMS IN GERMAN AGRICULTURE

By 1927 German farmers were finding it difficult to compete with cheap imports from abroad. Their debts mounted and their incomes shrank. The Nazis were quick to exploit this and began a systematic campaign to win the votes of angry farmers.

THE IMPACT OF THE WALL STREET CRASH

When the US stock market crashed (see Fact File) in October 1929, Germany's economic problems multiplied rapidly. US loans were stopped, which meant that German banks, state governments and **industrialists** were starved of the investment capital they needed. America's depression also reduced the amount of international trade so German export firms could not sell their goods abroad. Unemployment rose rapidly as shops, businesses, factories and workshops closed down.

industrialists
men who own large factories, mines, shipyards etc.

FACT FILE
THE WALL STREET CRASH

During the 1920s too many Americans had bought goods and shares on credit. By 1929 shares were changing hands for huge sums as their prices soared above their true value. In October 1929 the bubble burst when share prices suddenly tumbled. This became known as the Wall Street Crash, after New York's financial district. Thousands of individuals, many businesses and even banks were ruined. The crash affected Europe because Americans reduced the amount of goods they bought from abroad.

SPIRALLING PROBLEMS

Rising unemployment in Germany created a spiral of problems (see Source 2). The unemployed were unable to buy goods, which forced more businesses to close. Banks lost the money they had lent to bankrupt firms, so

people who had invested money in the banks withdrew it rapidly because they feared they would lose it altogether. This caused several German banks to collapse in 1931, making the situation even worse.

SOURCE 1   A dole queue in Hanover during the Depression.

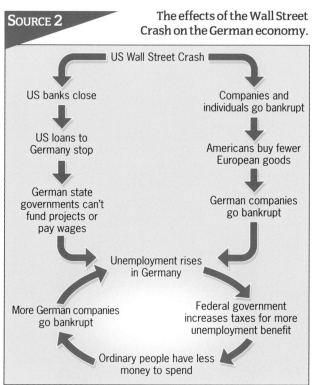

SOURCE 2   The effects of the Wall Street Crash on the German economy.

US Wall Street Crash

US banks close → US loans to Germany stop → German state governments can't fund projects or pay wages → Unemployment rises in Germany

Companies and individuals go bankrupt → Americans buy fewer European goods → German companies go bankrupt → Federal government increases taxes for more unemployment benefit → Ordinary people have less money to spend → More German companies go bankrupt → Unemployment rises in Germany

POLITICAL ISSUES

The depth of the economic crisis caused severe political problems. The government found itself faced with huge numbers of unemployed wanting benefit payments, but had much less tax income with which to pay them. In March 1930 the coalition government resigned because its ministers could not agree on how to deal with this problem. It proved impossible to form a new coalition that could command the support of the Reichstag. So President Hindenburg allowed the new Chancellor, Heinrich Bruening, to govern with emergency powers under Article 48 (see p16) of the Constitution. German democracy had broken down.

(see p16)

SOURCE 3

Hitler with Nazi deputies in the Reichstag, 1930.

THE NAZI BREAKTHROUGH

In September 1930, Bruening called an election to try to gain more support for his SPD-led coalition. But the result was a shock. The Nazis emerged as Germany's second biggest party with 107 seats. The KPD (Communists) also made gains and won 77 seats. These results made the economic situation even worse because foreigners, worried that Nazi gains would make Germany even more unstable, withdrew even more money from the country.

SOURCE 4
Reichstag seats won by Nazis and Communists in elections in 1930 and 1932.

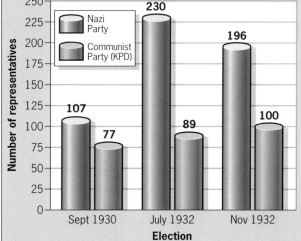

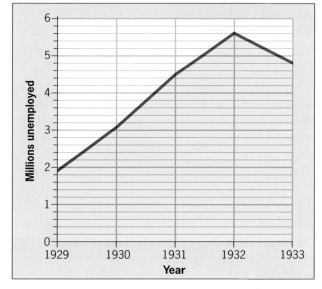

Unemployment in Germany, 1929-1933.

Questions

1. Study Sources 1 and 2. How do they show the seriousness of the Depression in Germany? Explain your answer.
2. Study Source 3. Why do you think the Nazi deputies wore their SA uniforms for Reichstag meetings?
3. Study Source 4. Why do you think both the Nazis and the Communists won support from the poorest people in Germany during the Depression?
4. How did the Depression affect Germany? Make your own notes on its effect on:
   • German international trade
   • farmers   • industry
   • banks   • workers

How did the Nazis come to power?

HOW DID THE NAZIS GAIN SUPPORT?

Who voted for the Nazis?

The remarkable feature of Nazi electoral success was that the Party won support from all social groups and classes. This was because Hitler stressed some simple themes that were reassuring to people facing turmoil and an uncertain future. He blamed all Germany's troubles on the men he called the 'November Criminals' – the Socialists who had agreed to surrender in 1918. He promised he would restore German unity and strength. The Nazis were particularly successful in winning support from rural communities, especially in Protestant areas of Germany. They also won the support of middle-class businessmen and professionals worried about the threat of communism. Young people, who blamed the older generation and the democratic system for Germany's problems, flocked to the Nazis. Even some members of the working class, most of whom stayed loyal to the SPD or KPD, were drawn to Hitler's promises to end class divisions and restore German greatness.

Propaganda

Josef Goebbels (see p46), who was in charge of Nazi propaganda, played a major part in winning over voters. The Party's propaganda output was relentless and not simply confined to election campaigns. Rallies and speeches were held all over Germany, and good speakers were given special training. They were encouraged to exploit local issues and promise solutions. Posters and leaflets were simple, effective and widespread. The party's newspaper emphasised the propaganda themes. When a young Nazi called Horst Wessel was murdered by Communists in 1929, Goebbels portrayed him as a martyr and the marching song composed in his honour became the Nazis' anthem.

Hitler's rallies

Hitler's speeches were also a major asset. By 1928 the ban on him speaking (see p30) had been lifted in all the German states. Hitler became the first major politician to use a plane and, during a single week in April 1932, he spoke at 20 different rallies, addressing over a million people. The tour was called 'The Führer over Germany'.

Political violence

The growing strength of the Nazis and the Communists increased the number and scale of their violent street clashes. The SA set about terrorising whole towns and provinces. Opposition parties had their offices burned, their meetings disrupted and prominent members beaten up. At times, the violence threatened to get out of hand, especially when five SA men were convicted of murdering a Communist in a Silesian village in 1932. Hitler did his best to blame the Communists for all the violence. He also claimed that the Nazis were the only party doing anything to stop them. There is no doubt that the violence lost the Nazis some middle-class votes, but it was also important in weakening and terrorising their opponents.

GERMAN POLITICS, 1930-1933

Heinrich Bruening had been Chancellor since March 1930. But his policies to tackle the economic crisis only made matters worse. He

SOURCE 1 A soup kitchen set up by the German army to feed the poor and unemployed, 1931.

Hitler greets President Hindenburg after his appointment as Chancellor in January, 1933.

increased taxes and cut the level of unemployment benefit and the salaries of government employees. This was because he believed that the government should not spend more than it received in tax revenue. This just added to the misery and, as more and more Germans became unemployed and destitute, Bruening was nicknamed the 'Hunger Chancellor'. Some of Hindenburg's advisers began to get worried about these policies. They feared that political and economic collapse could cause civil war and bring the Communists to power. In May 1932 Bruening was sacked and replaced by an unknown aristocrat called Franz von Papen.

Papen, Schleicher and the Nazis

Papen held a new election in July 1932. The Nazis made big gains and became Germany's largest party. Papen tried to get the Nazis to support him by offering Hitler the post of Vice-Chancellor. Hitler refused. He wanted complete power, or nothing. In November Papen called another election. The Nazis lost seats, partly because of SA violence, but Hitler still refused to join the government. Papen was replaced by another of Hindenburg's advisers, General Schleicher, who tried to split the NSDAP by offering the post of Vice-Chancellor to another leading Nazi. However, the offer was refused and Schleicher, too, resigned.

HITLER'S APPOINTMENT AS CHANCELLOR

Papen was so anxious to get back into power that he made a secret deal with Hitler. He agreed to persuade President Hindenburg to accept Hitler as Chancellor on the understanding that Papen would be Vice-Chancellor and that there would be only two other Nazis in the **cabinet**. Papen believed that he had got Hitler under control and that the Nazis would dutifully serve in a government dominated by members of Germany's conservative elite.

> **cabinet**
> the senior government ministers

On January 30, 1933, Hindenburg appointed Hitler Chancellor of Germany. A few days later, he received an angry letter from one of his former wartime colleagues who wrote: 'This accursed Hitler will cast our country into the abyss. Future generations will damn you in your grave for what you have done.' It was a remarkable prophecy.

Questions

1. How did Bruening's policies make Germany's problems worse?
2. Why were Papen and Schleicher anxious to enlist Hitler's support? Explain your answer.
3. 'Hindenburg made Hitler Chancellor in 1933 because he had no other choice.' Using the information and sources in this section, explain whether you agree with this statement.

The early years of Weimar Germany, 1919-23

In a GCSE History examination candidates are asked several types of questions. These include:

- The evaluation of sources
- The evaluation of sources using your own knowledge
- Writing extended answers using your own knowledge

A fourth type is the structured question. In this type of question candidates are asked to use only their own knowledge to write an answer. The answers are similar to extended writing answers but tend to be shorter.

QUESTIONS AND RACHEL'S ANSWERS

(a) What were the main reasons the Germans disliked the Treaty of Versailles?

(4 marks)

Article 231 caused many problems for the Germans. Accepting it meant the Germans took sole responsibility for starting the war. By accepting the War Guilt Clause it allowed the Allies to impose other destructive terms. The sum of £6.6 billion in reparations completely drained the Germans' economy. It was a sum they couldn't afford to pay. The Allies also made the Germans reduce their armed forces, leaving them weak and defenceless against any real threat.

(b) Explain why Germany experienced so much political and economic trouble in 1923.

(6 marks)

In January 1923 the French and Belgians invaded the Ruhr region in reaction to Germany's failure to pay reparations payments. This led to economic disaster because inflation increased when the government encouraged passive resistance and paid workers for it. The government printed money, causing its value to decrease, and this led to hyperinflation in Germany. Unemployment figures soared above six million. There was some political unrest due to the Nazi party, which was still provincial and small. The Munich Putsch led to civil unrest and saw the first political move from Hitler.

(c) 'The main reason Germany was stable between 1924 and 1929 was because of the work of Gustav Stresemann.' Do you agree with this statement? Explain your answer.

(10 marks)

Life in Germany improved a lot during the period 1924-1929. The German people calmed down and were stable. The Dawes Plan helped them because it reduced the amount of money Germany had to pay the Allies. This meant their industry could recover. They also did better abroad because they joined the League of Nations and signed the Locarno Treaty, which made them more stable. It was Stresemann who did this. The Young Plan was useful too and the American loans helped Germany to recover.

Question (a)

Candidates are expected to identify which parts of the Treaty of Versailles were disliked by Germany and why.

Rachel explains the Germans' dislike of the War Guilt Clause and the reparations. She also explains how the two are linked. She mentions the reduction of their armed forces, although she doesn't provide much detail about this.

However, she neglects to mention the loss of territory. This was especially important with the land in the east, which was lost to Poland. This was resented most in Germany, especially by the nationalists.

As a result, Rachel received 2 out of a possible 4 marks.

Question (b)

Candidates are expected to provide reasons for the political and economic turmoil of 1923. Marks will be given where **links** are made between the reasons.

For economic trouble, Rachel understands that the invasion of the Ruhr triggered the hyperinflation in Germany. She also understands that the German government's policy of supporting 'passive resistance' was also partly to blame for this. She is aware, too, that Hitler and the Nazi Party attempted a putsch that year. However, by referring to unemployment soaring to six million, she has got two separate crises confused. It was in the Depression of 1930-32, not 1923, that unemployment was the major problem.

For political trouble, Rachel's comments on Hitler's Munich (Beer Hall) Putsch are vague. Although she points out that the Nazi Party was still small in 1923, she does not actually mention that Hitler's putsch was unsuccessful. She could have pointed out that the Nazis were not the only people in Bavaria in 1923 trying to use the chaos of that year to attack the Weimar Republic.

As a result, Rachel received 4 out of a possible 6 marks.

Question (c)

Candidates are required to engage in some extended writing to explain whether or not Stresemann was chiefly responsible for the stability of Germany between 1924 and 1929. They must also give reasons for their answer.

Rachel has made some relevant points but doesn't really write enough to answer the question fully. It is important to write most for the answer that carries the largest number of marks. Rachel explains that the Dawes Plan helped the German economy, but her details are not quite accurate. The Dawes Plan reduced the size of each annual repayment, not the total amount to be paid. It was the Young Plan that reduced the overall total. Although she mentions the loans from the USA, she does not explain exactly how they helped recovery in Germany. She is right to give Stresemann credit for Germany joining the League of Nations and signing the Locarno Treaty, but she does not explain how these helped Germany or made the country more stable. Above all, she does not really answer the question about Stresemann. She needs to show that some reasons for Germany's recovery - such as the Dawes Plan and the American loans - were not entirely the work of Stresemann. She must contrast this with the achievements in foreign policy for which he does deserve the credit.

As a result of these problems, Rachel received only 3 out a possible 10 marks.

EXTENSION WORK

Which were more serious for the survival and stability of the Weimar Republic: its economic problems or its political difficulties? Explain your answer, **using information and sources from the last two chapters**.

(15 marks)

• OCR accepts no responsibility whatsoever for the accuracy or method of working in the anwers given.

Weimar Germany, 1924-1933

SOURCE A
From a GCSE textbook published in 1987.

Hitler had a true politician's ability to understand what the people wanted. He knew that the middle classes in Germany wanted stability and no repetition of the disaster of 1923 and that the workers wanted jobs and welfare benefits. He was also aware that the big industrialists and landowners wanted the trade union movement made powerless and the Communists crushed. He told all of these groups exactly what they wanted to hear. To the army, he offered massive expansion and new weapons. This meant that the officer corps was only too happy to support him.

SOURCE B
Hitler's comments on how he came to power, made in May 1942.

I considered it of the highest importance that I should legally take over the chancellorship with the blessing of President Hindenburg. Because it was only as a legally elected Chancellor that I would be able to overcome the opposition of all the other parties. If I had seized power illegally, the army might have tried to overthrow me.

QUESTIONS AND GIHAN'S ANSWERS

(a) What can you learn from **Source A** about Hitler's popularity in 1933?

(3 marks)

In 1933 Hitler had reached the height of his popularity. He used methods that would make Nazism appeal to all classes. Germany had been weakened by the Depression of the 1920s. Hitler used this to turn the people against other political and social groups, blaming them for the disaster to further his own cause. The people were happy to support him, persuaded by his powerful political speeches and propaganda. This was because he offered them what they wanted and what they had not had before.

(b) Using **Source A** and your own knowledge, explain why many middle-class Germans voted for Hitler in 1932.

(7 marks)

The Nazis won 107 seats in 1930 and then they went up to 230 in 1932. After that, they only got 196 seats. Lots of Germans voted for them because Hitler promised them what they wanted to hear. He promised that the middle classes would be stable and not have another crisis like in 1923. He told the workers they would get jobs and benefits and he told the rich people he would crush the Communists. Germans also wanted their army to be strong, so when Hitler promised them new weapons and expansion, they were pleased.

(c) How important was Hitler's political skill in assisting his rise to power? Use your own knowledge to explain your answer.

(15 marks)

Hitler was a very skilled politician and this was one of the major factors that brought him to power in 1933. In the early stages of his career his main contribution to the party was his ability as a speaker. This helped him a lot. First, he spoke to the few members of the NSDAP, but in the 1930s he spoke to thousands of people.

Not only his ability to speak, but also his ability to tell people exactly what they wanted to hear, made him a skilled politician and brought him to power in 1933. As it says in Source A, he had a true politician's ability to understand what people wanted.

Hitler was also clever in the way he kept the Nazi Party together. The SA wanted to seize power and he wanted to come to power legally. Hitler cleverly avoided a split in the Party over this. He was also skilful in the way he didn't allow himself to be used by Papen and the other conservatives. In fact, he used them!

All this combined to give him the mass support he needed to become Chancellor of Germany. I think that without his political skill he would not have been able to come to power in 1933.

Question (a)

Gihan correctly sees that the source emphasises Hitler's ability to appeal to all social groups in Germany and that this was one of the main reasons for his success. However, he makes the mistake of placing the Depression in the twenties. The Wall Street Crash did not occur until October 1929 and the severe crisis began in Germany in 1930. Gihan is also vague about how the source explains Hitler's ability to exploit the difficulties in Germany. He needs to show that the problems faced by each of the groups mentioned in Source A grew worse during the depression.

As a result, Gihan was awarded 1 out of a possible 3 marks.

Question (b)

Gihan's figures about the number of Nazis in the Reichstag are correct, but he does not relate them to the question. Not all the Germans who voted for the Nazis were middle-class. He uses the ideas in the source, but does not go beyond simply re-telling what the source says in brief. He needed to point out that the middle classes in Germany began to vote for the Nazis in large numbers because they were victims of the Depression. This was true of other groups, too. Middle-class people who ran their own businesses lost customers. Some lost their management jobs as big businesses and banks closed down. Most middle-class people were worried by the political violence of the Depression years and feared the growth of communism. They believed that the Nazis were the only party capable of dealing with the Communists and ending the disorder. Gihan needs to point out that the middle classes were particularly attracted to the Nazis because they offered unity and a restoration of German greatness. All of these themes can be seen in the source.

As a result, Gihan was awarded 2 out of a possible 7 marks.

Question (c)

Gihan correctly identifies Hitler's ability as a speaker as one of his main political skills and he uses the information in Source A to show how Hitler used this ability effectively. Gihan also mentions Hitler's skill in keeping the Party united and outmanoeuvring the conservatives.

However, he should have referred to some examples to support his argument. Finally, in assessing how important Hitler's skill was, Gihan needs to consider the other factors that enabled him to come to power. These include the impact of the Depression on German voters, and the impact of Nazi propaganda. He should have considered whether these factors were more or less important than Hitler's political skill.

As a result, Gihan was awarded 10 out of a possible 15 marks.

EXTENSION WORK

What role did each of the following play in bringing Hitler to power in 1933:
- The economic problems caused by the Depression
- Germany's political problems between 1930 and 1932
- The Nazi Party and its propaganda?

Explain your answer, **using information and sources from the last chapter**.

(15 marks)

• AQA accepts no responsibility whatsoever for the accuracy or method of working in the anwers given.

The destruction of the Constitution

HOW DID HITLER BECOME DICTATOR SO QUICKLY?

When Hitler became Chancellor, he did not appear to be in a strong position. There were only three Nazis, including himself, in his cabinet. The Nazi Party had won only a third of the votes at the last election, so there were plenty of Germans who did not support them. Hitler himself could be sacked at any time by the President. But, within 18 months, Hitler had destroyed the German Constitution and made himself a **dictator**. Why was this process so swift?

dictator
a ruler whose power is not restricted in any way

NAZI VIOLENCE

The key to Hitler's success was his ability to use (and abuse) his power as head of the government, in combination with the ruthless violence of the Nazi thugs against their political opponents. The violence began immediately – members of the SA beat up Socialists and Communists, or hauled them off to improvised prisons known as concentration camps. The offices of Nazi opponents were attacked. Their printing presses were smashed to prevent them publishing anti-Nazi newspapers, leaflets and posters. Well-known individuals and their families were intimidated. This violence was crucial in making people too frightened to oppose the Nazis. Source 1 shows how effective it was.

The police did little to stop the violence because most of them, even if they were not Nazis, disliked the Communists. In Prussia,

| SOURCE 1 | A letter from a senior member of the Socialist Party to a colleague, February 24, 1933. |

'Several of my meetings have been disrupted and a considerable section of the audience had to be taken away badly injured. I therefore request the cancellation of meetings with me as speaker. There is no longer any police protection against the aggressive actions of the SA and SS at my meetings.'

which was Germany's largest state and covered two-thirds of the country, the police were under the control of Hermann Goering, a leading Nazi. On February 22, 1933, he made the SA in Prussia into auxiliary policemen. This, in effect, made their violence legal.

HERMANN GOERING (1893-1946)
Goering was a daring and successful fighter pilot in the First World War. His distinguished background helped to make the Party respectable and gain them powerful and wealthy supporters. In 1933 Hitler put him in charge of the Prussian police and he ruthlessly intimidated the Nazis' opponents. In 1936 he took charge of preparing the German economy for war, but was only partially successful. He also commanded the Luftwaffe, but its failure to win the Battle of Britain in 1940 caused his power and influence to decline. He was tried as a war criminal by the Allies after the war, and committed suicide to escape being hanged.

HITLER'S 'LEGAL' REVOLUTION

However, to gain complete power Hitler needed a law that would enable him to change the Constitution and transfer the power to make laws from the Reichstag to himself. This was called an Enabling Law. This could only be achieved if two-thirds of the Reichstag voted in favour. So new elections were called for March 5, 1933. But before they could be held, a dramatic event occurred which Hitler exploited to the full.

THE REICHSTAG FIRE

During the evening of February 27, Hitler was having dinner with his propaganda chief, Josef Goebbels. They received a telephone call to say that the Reichstag building was ablaze. Hitler and Goebbels rushed to the scene, convinced that this was the start of an uprising by the Communists.

The next day, the aged President Hindenburg was persuaded by Hitler to issue an Emergency Decree giving Hitler sweeping powers to arrest anyone suspected of opposing the government. The violence against Communists and Socialists increased in intensity. By April, 25,000 had been arrested in Prussia alone. On election day in March 1933, the Nazis gained more seats but did not achieve a two-thirds majority (see Source 2).

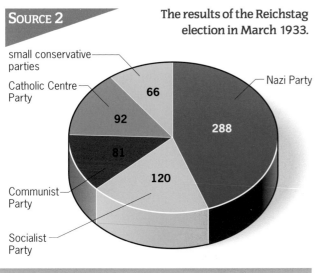

The results of the Reichstag election in March 1933.

- small conservative parties
- Catholic Centre Party — 92
- 66
- Nazi Party — 288
- 81
- 120
- Communist Party
- Socialist Party

THE ENABLING LAW

Hitler would now have to persuade other parties to support the Enabling Law. When the new parliament met in its temporary home at Potsdam (on the outskirts of Berlin), Goebbels staged a propaganda show to convince the German people that the Nazis were a respectable, traditional party, who aimed to restore German greatness.

On March 23 the Reichstag debated the Enabling Law. The small conservative parties had already agreed to vote in favour. The Emergency Decree was used to prevent the Communists from taking their seats. Hitler knew the Socialists would vote against the Law so he had only to win over the Catholic Centre Party in order to gain his two-thirds majority. The Catholics were subjected to a mixture of intimidation and persuasion. As the deputies arrived for the debate, they were surrounded by heavily armed SA men. Hitler spoke in the Reichstag and denounced the Socialists, but made generous promises to the Catholics (see Source 3). When the vote was taken, only the Socialists opposed the Enabling Law, and it was passed by 444 votes to 94.

SOURCE 3
From Hitler's speech to the Reichstag on the Enabling Law, March 23, 1933.

"My government regards both the Catholics and the Protestants as the most important factors for maintaining our society. The rights of the churches will not be touched. The government wants sincere co-operation between Church and State."

THE REMAINING OPPOSITION IS SWEPT ASIDE

Trade unions
Hitler announced that there would be a public holiday on May 1, and, on May 2, the SA occupied and closed down any trade union offices they had not already destroyed. German workers were now ordered to join the Nazis' own trade union – the German Labour Front (DAF).

The Pope
In July the Nazis signed an agreement with the Pope, known as the Concordat. The Catholics agreed to the abolition of the Centre Party in return for Hitler's promise that the Nazis would not interfere with Catholicism in Germany. Hitler was delighted because an agreement with the Pope gave him international prestige.

Germany becomes a one-party state
On July 14 a new law proclaimed that the Nazi Party was the only political party allowed in Germany. Most parties had seen what was coming and dissolved themselves anyway. The new regime called itself the Third Reich. According to the Nazis, the First Reich was the Holy Roman Empire, and the Second Reich was the old German Empire.

Questions

1. Study Source 1. How does it help explain the success of the Nazis' methods of frightening their opponents into co-operating with them?
2. Study Source 2. Why would the Enabling Law have been defeated if the Catholic Centre Party had joined the Socialists and voted against it?
3. What methods did Hitler use to become dictator so quickly? Draw two columns, labelled 'violent methods' and 'legal methods'. Which methods go where? Some may appear in both!

The Night of the Long Knives

ROEHM AND THE SA

By the summer of 1933 Hitler's political power was virtually complete. He now wanted a period of calm so that the German economy could recover from the depression. This meant that SA violence had to be brought under control. In August, they lost their status as auxiliary policemen. Roehm, the leader of the SA, was not pleased. He wanted a 'second revolution' in which loyal Nazis would replace Germany's conservatives in positions of wealth and power in the economy, the government, the judicial system and, above all, the armed forces. Roehm saw himself as the leader of a vast new German army, built around the SA.

Hitler totally disagreed with Roehm's ambitions for the SA. He wanted a professional army, not an SA rabble. He also knew that the army was the only institution powerful enough to obstruct his ambition of becoming President when Hindenburg died. The threat to Hitler from Roehm and the SA leaders was growing. However, Hitler was reluctant to remove Roehm, who was one of his oldest friends and colleagues.

SOURCE 2

The SA parading past Hitler in Hanover, 1933.

> **INVESTIGATE...**
> Who else wanted to see the end of the SA, and why? Go to
> www.spartacus.schoolnet.co.uk/GERsa.htm

THE PURGE OF THE SA LEADERSHIP

Hitler was forced to act when it became clear that Hindenburg did not have long to live. In the early hours of June 30, 1934, Hitler arrived at Roehm's holiday hotel in Bad Wiessee, a resort near Munich, and ordered his immediate arrest. Simultaneous arrests of other SA leaders took place in Berlin. There were no trials; those arrested were shot within hours. Roehm was shot by two SS men in his prison cell the following day. Possibly as many as 200 people were killed in the **purge**. This became known as the 'Roehm Purge' or the 'Night of the Long Knives'.

purge
to clean out, or get rid of something bad or impure

SOURCE 3 — Roehm's execution, described by the governor of the Munich prison where Roehm was being held.

'Two SS men were taken to Roehm's cell. They ordered him to shoot himself. If he did not comply, they would return in ten minutes and kill him. When the time was up, the two SS men re-entered the cell and found Roehm standing with his chest bared. Immediately one of them shot him in the throat, and Roehm collapsed on the floor. Since he was still alive, he was killed with a shot, point blank, through the temple. The bullet not only penetrated his skull, but also the ceiling of the cell below.'

SOURCE 4 — An account by a German Socialist on the reactions of ordinary Germans to the Night of the Long Knives.

'Hitler's courage in taking decisive action has made him a hero. He has won strong approval and sympathy. People think his action is proof that he wants order and decency. Reports from different parts of the country are unanimous that people are expressing satisfaction that Hitler has acted so decisively.'

'FÜHRER OF THE GERMAN REICH AND PEOPLE'

When Hindenburg died on August 2, Hitler combined the offices of Chancellor and President. The army agreed to a new oath of loyalty to Hitler personally as 'Führer of the German Reich and people'. The purge helped the SS, led by Heinrich Himmler, take a big step towards becoming Germany's police force. The SS now took control of the concentration camps that had been set up by the SA immediately after Hitler came to power in 1933. Hitler's personal popularity soared after the Night of the Long Knives. Most Germans feared and disliked the corruption of the SA and were glad its power had been curbed.

Questions

1. Study Source 1. How does it help you to understand why Hitler felt threatened by Roehm?
2. Study Source 2. How does it help you to understand why the German army were worried about the SA?
3. What does Source 3 reveal about the ruthlessness of Hitler and the SS?
4. Study Source 4. Why do you think ordinary Germans believed that Roehm's murder would help to restore 'order and decency'? Explain your answer.
5. Write a brief set of notes to explain how each of the following benefited from the Night of the Long Knives.
   * Hitler
   * Himmler and the SS
   * The German army

How was Nazi Germany governed?

WHAT WAS HITLER'S PERSONAL ROLE?

Hitler was an all-powerful Führer whose word was law. But he did not take all the decisions in the Nazi government. He was personally lazy, especially about paperwork, and left much of the routine business of government to others. Often significant policies were implemented without much reference to him. Nevertheless, his subordinates understood the kind of policies they were expected to follow, and Hitler still interfered from time to time if he thought it necessary to do so.

Hitler did personally direct Germany's foreign policy and the conduct of the war because these were the two areas that interested him most. His reluctance to bother himself with the ordinary details of government allowed some of his more ruthless subordinates to make themselves extremely powerful. For example, Goering accumulated considerable power over the economy. No one, however, ever became strong enough to challenge Hitler because they all depended on him for their power. The decline of Goering's influence after his air force failed to win the Battle of Britain in 1940 shows that Hitler could undermine even his most prominent subordinates.

HEINRICH HIMMLER (1900-1945)

After service as an officer cadet in the First World War, Himmler joined the Nazis and took part in the Munich (Beer Hall) Putsch. He then had an unsuccessful career as a poultry farmer before taking command of Hitler's bodyguard – the SS – in 1929. He rapidly expanded it into an elite police force with its own secret agents. He took control of the Gestapo in 1934 and Hitler rewarded him for organising the Night of the Long Knives by making him Chief of the German Police in 1936. During the Second World War Himmler implemented Hitler's plans for ethnic cleansing in Eastern Europe and organised the systematic murder of the Jews, known as the Holocaust.

THE POLICE STATE

The SS
The job of making sure there was no opposition to Nazi rule was given to the SS. When it was formed in 1925, the SS had been nothing more than Hitler's personal bodyguard. But Heinrich Himmler, who became its leader in 1929, developed it into the Party's own police force. In 1932 he established the SD (*Sicherheitsdienst* – security service) as the secret intelligence service of the SS.

The Gestapo
Once Hitler was in power, the SS took control of the Prussian Secret State Police (*Geheimestaatspolizie* – Gestapo) in 1934. Himmler's deputy, Reinhard Heydrich, expanded the Gestapo into a nationwide organisation to hunt down any Germans who opposed the regime and its policies.

CONCENTRATION CAMPS

Anyone arrested by the Gestapo could be held indefinitely in 'protective custody' in a concentration camp. The number of prisoners fluctuated considerably. When the camps were first established there were as many as 100,000 prisoners. These were mostly political opponents. Numbers dwindled quickly because fewer people were prepared to oppose the regime as it consolidated its power. The number of prisoners rose again in 1938 to about 60,000 when the Gestapo began rounding up people regarded as 'asocial'. This category included gypsies, homosexuals, Jehovah's Witnesses, beggars and tramps. Once the Second World War began, the numbers shot up further. By 1945 as many as 1,300,000 people had endured a period of 'protective custody'.

The camps were run by SS guards (*Totenkopfverbande* – Death's Head Units) who were trained to be ruthless, brutal and inhumane. Punishments were severe. Minor offences were punished with beatings, and anything the guards regarded as political opposition could result in execution. In

Concentration camp badges for different categories of prisoners.

Kennzeichen für Schutzhäftlinge in den Konz.Lagern

Form und Farbe der Kennzeichen

	Politisch	Berufs-Verbrecher	Emigrant	Bibel-forscher	Homo-sexuell	Asozial
Grund-farben	▼	▼	▼	▼	▼	▼
Abzeichen für Rückfällige	▼	▼	▼	▼	▼	▼
Häftlinge der Straf-kompanie	▼⦿	▼⦿	▼⦿	▼⦿	▼⦿	▼⦿
Abzeichen für Juden	✡	✡	✡	✡	✡	✡

Besondere Abzeichen					Beispiel
✡ Jüd. Rasse-schänder	✡ Rasse-schänderin	⦿ Flucht-verdächtigt	2307 Häftlings-Nummer	
▼P Pole	▼T Tscheche	▲ ehemaliger Wehrmacht Angehöriger	⬤ Häftling Ia	

CONCENTRATION CAMPS

As soon as Hitler came to power, the SA began rounding up the Nazis' political enemies and putting them in hastily constructed prison camps. After the Night of the Long Knives, the SS took control of these camps and ran them with brutal efficiency. During the war, new camps, usually with labour camps attached, were set up so that the SS could make the prisoners work for them. Most of the wartime prisoners were foreigners from the conquered territories. By 1944, Germany and its conquered territories had 20 concentration camps with 165 labour camps attached and 225,000 prisoners.

A typical punishment at Buchenwald concentration camp.

October 1937, ten prisoners at Buchenwald were drowned in a cesspool full of excrement.

The SS camps were established near factories or quarries so that the inmates could be forced to work. The concentration camps became part of a vast SS economic empire involved in quarrying, brick making, forestry, clothing, furniture and even soft drinks. By 1939 the SS had become a state within a state.

Regulations for discipline and punishment in the concentration camps, drawn up by the SS Inspector-General of the Camps.

'Toleration means weakness. Punishment will be mercilessly handed out whenever the interests of the Fatherland warrant it. All punishments will be recorded on files. If a prisoner attempts to escape, he is to be shot without warning.'

Questions

1. Study Source 1. Can you understand any of the prisoner categories? What does it reveal about the SS's range of camp intake?
2. How did the concentration camps help the SS to become so powerful in Nazi Germany?
3. How important was terror in running the state of Nazi Germany? Explain your answer, using information and sources in this section.

The propaganda machine

WHY WAS PROPAGANDA IMPORTANT?

The Nazis did not rely solely on fear and brutality to stay in power. Hitler believed that propaganda had a vital role to play in persuading the German people to accept Nazi ideas and in binding them together in a People's Community (*Volksgemeinschaft* – see p50).

Josef Goebbels, who had run the Party's electoral propaganda so brilliantly, was appointed Minister of Propaganda in March 1933. He immediately set about ridding German cultural life of books, ideas and people that did not accept Nazi philosophy. On May 10, 1933, libraries and bookshops were plundered for any titles the Nazis disliked. These were then burned in huge bonfires in the middle of university cities.

SOURCE 1 Hitler with children on his 50th birthday, April 20, 1939.

SOURCE 2 Hitler's propaganda theory, adapted from *Mein Kampf*.

'Most people can absorb very little information and their intelligence is small, but their power of forgetting is enormous. Therefore all effective propaganda must be limited to a very few points. It must constantly repeat these slogans until every member of the public understands what you want him to understand.'

JOSEF GOEBBELS (1897-1945)

Goebbels suffered from polio as a child and this left him with a crippled foot and a bitter, cynical personality. He joined the Nazis in 1925 and was put in charge of the Party organisation in Berlin. He had a flair for eye-catching, exciting propaganda and played an important part in making Hitler a national figure during the election campaigns of 1932. During the Third Reich he was Propaganda Minister, controlling all branches of the media and arts, helping to maintain Hitler's image and popularity. The day after Hitler's suicide, he poisoned his six children and killed himself and his wife.

HOW DID GOEBBELS CONTROL THE MEDIA?

Reich Chamber of Culture

In September 1933, Goebbels established the Reich Chamber of Culture, with departments for literature, press, radio, theatre, music and the creative arts. Membership was compulsory for anyone wanting to work in any of these fields. This meant that artists censored their own work, knowing that, if they did not, they would lose their membership. Hundreds of talented musicians, artists, film-makers and actors, many of them Jewish, left Germany because they were unacceptable to the Chamber of Culture.

Radio

Goebbels also worked hard to make sure ordinary Germans received the Nazi message. He arranged for 6,000 loudspeakers to be set up in public places so that everyone could hear government announcements. Cheap radios were manufactured. By 1941 the number of German homes with a radio had risen from four million to 16 million and listeners were given a mixture of drama, light music and political propaganda (see Source 3). Although listening to foreign broadcasts did not become illegal until the Second World War started, Goebbels ordered manufacturers to ensure that the cheap radios had narrow wave bands so that listeners could hear only German stations.

Cinema

A similar mixture of entertainment and politics dominated the cinema output of the Third Reich. The most popular films were escapist romances or adventures. Purely propaganda films were not successful at the box office because they were too crude. Only Leni Riefenstahl's famous film of the 1934 Party rally, *Triumph of the Will*, has been recognised as a cinematic masterpiece.

Newspapers and magazines

There were 3,500 newspapers and 10,000 magazines in Germany in 1933. Many were bought up by the Nazis during the 1930s. The Propaganda Ministry controlled the news agencies that provided them with their information, and all journalists had to join the Chamber of Culture.

Every September from 1933 to 1938 the Party held a mass rally in Nuremberg. These huge events, which lasted for several days, were designed not only to glorify the power and success of the regime, but also to make the Germans feel part of it. They were a mixture of religious ceremony, community festival, military parade and propaganda triumph.

SOURCE 4

Workers, with their spades carried like rifles, marching through Nuremberg on their way to the 1935 Party Rally.

SOURCE 3

NAZI PROPAGANDA POSTERS

'On the radio we hear music. We hear drums. We hear: Sieg Heil!… We hear the song: 'Germany, Germany above all else', and the song: 'Fly the flag'!'

Am Radio.
. Wir hören Musik.
Wir hören die Trommel.
.Wir hören: Sieg Heil!
Sieg Heil! Sieg Heil!
.Wir hören das Lied:
Deutschland, Deutschland
über alles,
. und das Lied:
Die Fahne hoch!
29
Trommel   Fahne

'March 13, 1938. One people, one empire, one leader.'

13·MÄRZ 1938
EIN VOLK EIN REICH
EIN FÜHRER

Questions

1. *Study Source 1. Why do you think this photograph was taken?*
2. *Study Source 3. What can you learn about Nazi propaganda from these posters?*
3. *Study Source 4. What does it tell you about the annual Nazi Party Rally in Nuremberg?*
4. *Study Source 2. How does Hitler's propaganda theory support Sources 1 and 3?*
5. *Why do you think propaganda was so important to the Nazis? Explain your answer, using information and sources in this section.*

EDEXCEL
style

The Nazi dictatorship

SOURCE A

From the *Volkischer Beobachter*, the official Nazi newspaper, March 1933.

The first concentration camp will be opened within the next few days and will hold 5,000 prisoners. All Communists and Social Democrats who endanger state security will be imprisoned. The police and the Ministry of the Interior are convinced that they are acting in the national interest and that these measures will have a distinct effect upon the whole nation.

SOURCE B

A photograph showing an SA policeman arresting suspected Communists, 1933.

SOURCE C

From the law passed in July 1933, which ended the existence of opposition parties in Germany.

Article 1: The National Socialist Workers' Party shall be the only party in Germany.

Article 2: Anyone who organises another political party shall be imprisoned and will serve between six months and three years.

SOURCE D

From a book by a former Nazi official, written in 1940. He left Germany in 1934. In this extract he reports a conversation he had with Roehm in 1934. He also said that Roehm was drunk at the time.

Adolf is a swine. He is betraying all of us now. He is becoming friendly with the army generals. Adolf knows what I want, I've told him often enough. We are revolutionaries, aren't we? The generals are a lot of old stick in the muds. I am the centre of the new army, don't they see that?

SOURCE E

Date	No. of Members
1929	30,000
1930	60,000
Jan 1931	100,000
Jan 1932	290,941
Aug 1932	445,279
Jan 1933	425,000
Mar 1933	2.5 million

SA members, 1924-1933.

QUESTIONS AND SAM'S ANSWERS

(a) Study **Source A**.

What can you learn from it about government attitudes towards political opponents in Nazi Germany?

(4 marks)

> Source A shows that the Nazi government quickly took a zero tolerance attitude towards opposition, in order to consolidate their own position of power. As described in this source, political opponents of the Nazis were placed in concentration camps, showing that the government saw them as a potential threat to the regime.

(b) Study **Sources A**, **B** and **C**.

Does **Source C** support the evidence of **Sources A** and **B**? Explain your answer.

(4 marks)

> Source C does support the evidence of Sources A and B because all three sources show the way in which the Nazis dealt with their political opponents. They all agree that those suspected of being opposed to the Nazi government were rounded up and arrested to remove the possibility of them forming serious competition. Source C shows how it eventually became illegal to form another political party. It highlights the fact that the Nazis had established a dictatorship in which any political or moral beliefs that contradicted those of the Nazis were to be eradicated.

(c) Study **Sources D** and **E**.

How useful are these two sources as evidence about the threat to Hitler posed by the SA?

(8 marks)

> Source D shows more clearly than Source E that Hitler had enemies within the SA. This is because Roehm is speaking directly against him and implying that Roehm and the SA would threaten Hitler's position of power. It shows that Roehm did not like the generals, and they put pressure on Hitler to get rid of Roehm. Source E is useful because it shows how many men there were in the SA.

(d) Study **all the Sources**. 'Hitler secured control of Germany by August 1934 because he had the support of the army.' Use these sources, and your own knowledge, to explain whether you agree with this view.

(12 marks)

> Hitler was ruthless and put lots of people in prison as Source B shows. The army liked this because they did not like German communists. Therefore, the army supported Hitler. Soon all Hitler's opponents were in camps (Source A) and they were not allowed to form any other parties (Source C). When Roehm wanted to make the SA replace the army, Hitler had him killed in the Night of the Long Knives, which the army rejoiced about. They soon let him become Führer because, when Hindenburg died, Hitler became President as well. Hitler broke his promise to the army that they could be the only ones with weapons because he allowed the SS (bodyguards) to form armed units. This shows that he didn't always have the support of the army.

HOW TO SCORE FULL MARKS: WHAT THE EXAMINERS SAY

Question (a)
Candidates are required to select and interpret information from a written source to show government attitudes to political opposition in Nazi Germany.

Sam correctly observes that Source A shows how quickly the Nazis set up their concentration camps and that they were rapidly filled with political opponents. She could have pointed out that the first inmates were left-wing opponents (Communists and Socialists). Also that the Nazis correctly assumed the arrests would destroy opposition, and would be popular with the rest of the population. She could also have commented on the scale of the arrests, with the camps expected to hold as many as 5,000 prisoners.

As a result, Sam received 2 out of a possible 4 marks.

Question (b)
Candidates are required to compare and contrast the evidence of three sources, and decide whether one supports the others. They must give reasons for their answer.

Sam points out that all three sources show how the Nazis used tough laws to deal with their opponents and potential opponents. But she should have stressed the contrasts as well as the

similarities. *Although she hints that Source C is concerned with preventing future opposition from anyone, she needed to state that Sources A and B are concerned only with left-wing opponents.*

As a result, Sam received 3 out of a possible 6 marks.

Question (c)
Candidates are required to consider the usefulness of two sources, in relation to a particular issue.

Sam understands the two sources and shows that Roehm's complaints about the generals and the size of the SA both posed threats to Hitler. However, she needs to make her points more forcefully. Source E shows how rapidly the SA grew, especially after Hitler became Chancellor; by March 1933 it was an enormous force posing a considerable threat. Sam also needs to consider the origin of the sources, especially Source D. The author was a former Nazi who had left Germany in 1934, so might not be a wholly reliable source. His book was written six years after the conversation. Finally, how useful were Roehm's words if he was drunk at the time he made them?

As a result, Sam received 3 out of a possible 8 marks.

Question (d)
Candidates are required to use all five sources and their own knowledge to support their opinion on a particular issue.

Sam mentions most of the relevant factors in her answer. The Nazis' ruthless treatment of opponents was a major reason why Hitler secured total control of Germany. She also correctly points out that the army supported the Night of the Long Knives and that Hitler broke his promise to them by creating armed SS units. But Sam also needs to mention the legal powers (the Emergency and Enabling Law) used by the Nazis and the popularity of their actions with the German people. Finally, she could have referred to Source D, which confirms the view that the Army supported Hitler.

As a result, Sam was awarded 7 out of a possible 12 marks.

EXTENSION WORK

Which was more important in enabling the Nazis to establish their dictatorship: the violence used against their opponents or the legal powers that Hitler obtained? Explain your answer, **using information and sources from the last chapter**.

(15 marks)

• Edexcel accepts no responsibility whatsoever for the accuracy or method of working in the anwers given.

• Edexcel Modern European and World History (Syllabus A), 1999.

What was the People's Community?

The Nazis aimed to put their socialism into practice by creating a national People's Community (*Volksgemeinschaft*) of all Germans, whatever their background. They would all be united under Hitler's leadership.

THE GERMAN LABOUR FRONT AND 'BEAUTY OF LABOUR'

The Nazis knew that they had won as much support from the working class before 1933 as other groups in German society. This is why they were quick to destroy the free trade unions and replace them with the German Labour Front (DAF), led by Robert Ley. The DAF was designed to control the workers, but also set out to win their support. Ley established the 'Beauty of Labour' organisation to campaign for better factory working conditions.

'STRENGTH THROUGH JOY'

Ley also created the 'Strength through Joy' movement (*Kraft durch Freude* – KdF). This brought even the leisure time of the workers under the regime's control, and made luxury items, such as cars or holidays, available to ordinary people. The subsidised KdF holidays were undoubtedly popular (see Source 2). Even ordinary workers could take advantage of cheap railway fares, country holidays, weekend excursions, theatre trips and sports courses.

A Nazi poster promoting the *Volksgemeinschaft*, **1938.**

SOURCE 2

Germans holidaying at Wannsee, a lake outside Berlin, as part of the 'Strength through Joy' movement.

VOLKSWAGEN: THE PEOPLE'S CAR

In May 1938 Hitler laid the foundation stone for the Volkswagen factory which was supposed to produce a cheap 'people's car' (the English translation of *volkswagen*). More than 330,000 people invested 280 million Reichsmarks in the special savings scheme to buy one, but the factory switched to war production in 1940, and no VWs were produced until 1946.

Like the Volkswagen, the Nazis' aim of creating a classless society did not get very far because Hitler regarded fighting the war and destroying his racial enemies as more important (see p58). Nazi economic policies reinforced Germany's **capitalist social structure** and had much more impact on German society than the KdF.

capitalist social structure
a society in which the owners of businesses, industries, banks, etc., have the most power and influence

REACTIONS TO THE PEOPLE'S COMMUNITY

Many Germans at the time appreciated what the Nazis were achieving during the 1930s. Political turbulence had ended, the economy was recovering and Germany's international prestige improved. On the other hand, everyone was aware of the power of the Gestapo, and Himmler boasted about the tough conditions in the concentration camps. Many local Nazi bosses exploited their power and position to make themselves rich, and this made the Party, though not Hitler, unpopular. The Nazis' rigid demands for conformity annoyed many middle-class professionals, and farmers were soon grumbling again because their problems were not solved (see p64).

Few of the workers who had supported the KPD and the SPD before 1933 were won over to the Nazi cause. Although it was impossible for any left-wing groups to form, let alone challenge the regime, there is plenty of evidence (see Source 4, for example) to show that they remained loyal to their ideals and to their friends. Discussion groups and mutual

SOURCE 3

Hitler in a Volkswagen, 1939.

SOURCE 4 — A Gestapo report from the mid-1930s.

'Socialists don't have any formal organisations, but they meet over a glass of beer or keep in touch by means of family visits. They talk about the political situation and exchange news. They engage in whispering campaigns, which, at the moment, are their most effective illegal work against the state and the Nazi Party.'

support networks existed throughout the Third Reich, even though the working class was subject to more surveillance by the Gestapo than any other group.

Questions

1. Study Source 1. What can you learn from it about the kind of 'people's community' the Nazis wanted?
2. Study Source 2. How useful is it as evidence about the popularity of the KdF?
3. Study Source 3. Why do you think Hitler would have wanted this photograph published?
4. Study Source 4. What does it reveal about the strength of socialism in Nazi Germany?
5. 'The Nazis used the 'People's Community' to control, rather than to improve, the lives of the German people.' Do you agree with this statement? Use information and sources from this section to give reasons for your answer.

Youth and education

Hitler and the Nazis placed considerable emphasis on the education of young people. The Third Reich was intended to last for 1,000 years, so future generations needed careful training. The Nazis had formed their own youth movement – the Hitler Youth (*Hitler Jugend* or HJ) – as early as 1926, and by 1933 it had about 50,000 members.

Membership then increased steadily as the Nazis brought all other youth movements, apart from those run by Roman Catholics, under their control. The Hitler Youth Law of December 1, 1936, announced that 'all German young people, apart from being educated at home and at school, will be educated in the Hitler Youth physically, **intellectually**, and morally in the spirit of National Socialism to serve the nation and the community'. But membership did not become compulsory until March 1939.

intellectually
to do with thinking, reasoning and brain power

SOURCE 2 BDM girls exercising in Coburg, 1935.

seem to matter. However, the emphasis on physical fitness and military training did not appeal to everyone. Like the boys, girls were expected to join a junior movement at the age of ten and move onto the main organisation, the *Bund Deutscher Mädel* (League of German Maidens; see Source 2), at the age of 14. There was a similar emphasis on outdoor activities and physical fitness, together with practical training in how to be a wife and mother.

Towards the end of the Second World War, many Hitler Youth boys were enrolled into an SS tank division. They fought in France in 1944 and in the final defence of Berlin in 1945.

SOURCE 1 Hitler Youth boys giving the Nazi salute.

WHAT WAS THE HITLER YOUTH?

Boys were expected to join the *Jungvolk* (Young Folk) at the age of ten. At 14 they became members of the *Hitler Jugend* (Hitler Youth; see Source 3). Many enjoyed HJ activities, such as camping and hiking (see Source 3). Children from poorer homes experienced country holidays for the first time, and many of them were pleased that their class background did not

SOURCE 3 From the memoirs of a former member of the Hitler Youth.

'What I liked about the Hitler Youth was the comradeship. We often went off into the countryside, collected wood, made a fire and then cooked soup on it. It always made a deep impression on me to sit in the evening round a fire and sing songs and tell stories. These were probably our happiest hours in the Hitler Youth. Later, when I became a leader, I found the requirement of absolute obedience unpleasant. The Hitler Youth preferred that people should not have a will of their own.'

WARTIME DISENCHANTMENT

Once the war began in 1939, the number of young people who disliked the Hitler Youth grew. The organisation lost its best leaders to military service, and wartime restrictions reduced the range of its activities. Some youngsters opted out altogether and joined gangs who listened to banned music, hung around with girls and picked fights with Hitler Youth members. This trend worried the government so much that the ring-leaders of a gang in Cologne were publicly hanged in November 1944.

SCHOOLS AND UNIVERSITIES

The Nazis were quick to remove school and university teachers who did not agree with their ideas. Schools were subject to constant interference by the Hitler Youth, whose members were encouraged to reject their teachers' authority. Textbooks, especially in biology, history and German, were re-written to suit Nazi theories (see Source 4). Not surprisingly, many teachers became disillusioned. The school system was also disrupted by the SS and Hitler Youth, who took the best pupils into their own schools to train them as the next generation of Nazi leaders. Because the Nazis despised intellectual education, the number of students at university fell by 50 per cent between 1933 and 1939.

SOURCE 4

A question in a school mathematics textbook. Hitler believed that the mentally ill should be exterminated because they would weaken the German race (see p58).

asylum
a special hospital, usually for mentally ill patients

The construction of a lunatic **asylum** costs 6 million Reichsmarks. How many houses at 15,000 Reichsmarks could be built for that amount?

. . . . FACT FILE . . . .

NAZI LAWS ON YOUTH

In 1940 a new law banned anyone under 18 from the streets after dark. They were not allowed into restaurants, bars or cinemas after 9pm unless accompanied by an adult. Nor could they smoke in public. Girls under 21 were discouraged from wearing make-up, short dresses or high-heeled shoes. Some girls who disobeyed had their heads shaved as punishment.

SOURCE 5

Hitler's views on education.

From *Mein Kampf*:

'The racial state must base its educational work on the development of healthy bodies. Only in second place comes the training of mental faculties.'

From a speech, December 1938:

"German youth of the future must be slim and slender, swift as the greyhound, tough as leather, and hard as steel."

! INVESTIGATE...
Why was Hitler so desperate to control Germany's youth? Go to www.bbc.co.uk/education/modern/nazi/nazifla.htm

Questions

1. Why did some young people enjoy the Hitler Youth? Use the information and sources in this section to explain your answer.
2. Study Sources 1 and 2. In what ways do they show that Hitler's ideas for the education of young German people (Source 5) were put into practice?
3. Study Source 4. Why do you think the mathematics question has been written in this way?
4. Why do you think the Nazis placed more emphasis on physical fitness than on encouraging people to think for themselves?

Nazi policy towards women

Hitler had clear ideas about women. He believed that nature had given men and women different roles in life. The man's job was to work and fight. The woman's role was to look after the home and have children. The role of women in Nazi society was summed up in the slogan 'Kinder, Kirche, Küche' ('Children, Church, Kitchen'). These were the three things that women were expected to concern themselves with. It followed that women had no role to play in politics.

SOURCE 1   Hitler explains the role of women in the Third Reich.

'If the man's world is the State, his struggle, his readiness to devote his powers to the service of the community, the woman has a smaller world. For her world is her husband, her family, her children, and her home. What would become of the greater world if there were no one to tend and care for the smaller one?'

MARRIAGE, SEX AND CHILDREN

The Nazis wanted German mothers to produce more children. The birth rate had been dropping in many western European countries since the First World War mainly because contraception had become cheap and more readily available. This fall was particularly evident in Germany. In 1900 approximately two million German children were born, but in 1933 the figure was below one million. The Nazis feared that Germany might soon be swamped by people from Eastern Europe, whom they regarded as inferior. This is why even sex became a political issue in the Third Reich. As soon as they came to power the Nazis clamped down on abortion and made it harder to obtain contraceptives.

In June 1933 a marriage loan scheme was introduced. Couples received an interest-free loan of 600 RM (about four months' worth of an average worker's salary), the wife was required to give up her job and a quarter of the loan was cancelled for every child born. Propaganda constantly stressed the nobility of motherhood, and in 1939 the Mother's Cross was introduced to reward mothers of large families. The Nazis also set up a training organisation to run courses for women on how to run a home and motherhood. By 1938 it had a membership of four million.

Both the number of marriages and the birth rate increased, but Nazi policies were not primarily responsible for this. People made decisions about family size mainly for economic reasons. Nazi propaganda probably did no more than reinforce their decisions.

SOURCE 2   The number of births and marriages in Germany in the 1930s.

WOMEN IN WORK

The Nazis wanted women to give up their jobs and stay at home. This would help to solve the problems of unemployment for men. However, the number of working women actually increased during the 1930s. This was mainly because there was a serious shortage of farm workers in the countryside. One young girl, who advertised in a newspaper for a job, received 130 offers. Jobs for women also became available as the economy expanded and more men were called up for military service. Some women did leave their jobs to stay at home. But it is unlikely that they were responding to propaganda. As the German economy recovered, more families with a husband in a well-paid job could afford to support an unpaid housewife.

A painting by Adolf Wissel showing an idealized Nazi worker's family, 1939.

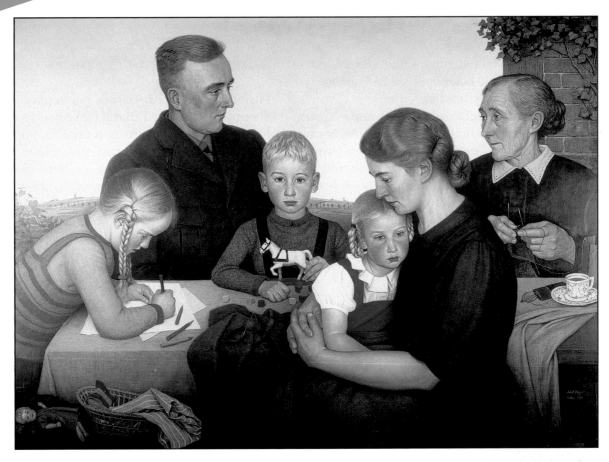

Women in regular paid employment

Year	Numbers (millions)
1925	4.2
1928	7.4
1933	4.8
1936	5.6
1939	7.1

FACT FILE

TROUSER TROUBLE

During the Second World War there was a fierce dispute among Nazi leaders about whether women should be allowed to wear trousers. Some believed that trousers were necessary for the kind of war-work women were doing, but one army officer banned his men from going out in public with women wearing them. Goebbels thought women should be allowed to wear trousers in winter; Hitler's views on the matter are not known.

Questions

1. Study Sources 1 and 3.
   a) In what ways do they support each other?
   b) How useful are they as evidence about life for women in Nazi Germany?

2. Study Sources 2 and 4. Do they suggest that Nazi policies towards women were successful?

3. Were women second-class citizens in Nazi Germany? Explain your answer using information and sources from this section.

The Churches and the Third Reich

humility
being modest about your own importance

The Christian Churches should have been opposed to Nazism. The Christian virtues of gentleness, **humility**, and concern for others clashed with the Nazi belief that life was a struggle and that only the fittest should survive. Furthermore, it should have been impossible to worship Jesus – a Jew – and accept Nazi anti-Semitism. But the Churches offered very little opposition to the Nazis. This was partly because Hitler deliberately did not tell them his real views about Christianity, but also because they shared some of the Nazis' ideas.

HITLER'S ATTITUDE TO THE CHURCHES

Hitler despised Christianity, but kept quiet about it. He realised that if he spoke his mind he would lose too many potential supporters. Most Germans were Christian, so Hitler made sure that the Party's 1920 programme claimed that the Nazis stood for 'positive Christianity'. This was a deliberately vague idea because Hitler wanted to appeal to both Catholics and Protestants without losing the support of either. He also knew that the Nazi Party's opposition to communism would guarantee Church support. The Churches hated and feared communism because of its **atheism**. Nevertheless, the Nazis wanted total control over all aspects of German life. This meant they were bound to try to control the Churches.

atheism
the belief that there is no God

> **SOURCE 2** Hitler's private views about Christianity, as told to his inner circle of admirers and friends in July 1941.
>
> *"The heaviest blow that ever struck humanity was the coming of Christianity. Communism is Christianity's illegitimate child. Both are inventions of the Jew."*

THE NAZIS' ATTEMPT TO CONTROL THE PROTESTANT CHURCHES

Two-thirds of German Christians were Protestants, but they belonged to a variety of different **sects**. In 1933, a small but determined set of Nazis calling themselves 'German Christians' tried to unite these Protestant groups under a single bishop. They succeeded in getting their candidate elected but, when they tried to re-write the Bible to remove its Jewish elements, they provoked opposition.

sect
a religious group whose beliefs differ slightly from those of others in the same religion

SOURCE 1

JUDENTUM

FREIMAUREREI

JESUITENTUM

Sie find entlarvt!

'Found out at last!' An SA man discovers a Jew, a Jesuit, and a Freemason hiding. From a Nazi student newspaper, 1935.

Protestant opposition

In October 1934 a determined Protestant pastor called Martin Niemoller set up a separate 'Confessional Church'. The Nazis did not ban it because it was too popular. But they did harass individuals. Niemoller himself was arrested in 1937 and released from Dachau only at the end of the war. A few courageous pastors believed that their faith compelled them to oppose the Nazi regime. The best known of these was Dietrich Bonhoeffer, who helped Jews to escape. He joined the opposition to Hitler. He was arrested in 1943 and executed a few days before the end of the war.

THE ROMAN CATHOLIC CHURCH

Initially, Hitler treated the Catholics with caution. Although only a third of German Christians were Catholic, they had their own political party whose votes he needed to pass the Enabling Law. Unlike the Protestants, few Catholics had voted for the Nazis.

The Concordat

In July 1933 Hitler's government signed a Concordat with the Roman Catholic Church. The Nazis agreed to respect the Catholics' freedom to worship and promised not to interfere with their schools and youth clubs. In return, Catholic priests were forbidden to take part in politics.

DIETRICH BONHOEFFER (1906-1945)

Bonhoeffer was a leading Protestant who became convinced that it was his Christian duty to oppose the Nazi government. He was a member of the Confessional Church that had been set up in 1934 to oppose the Nazis' attempts to interfere with the Protestants' freedom to worship. He assisted Jews to escape from Germany and, in 1942, helped Hitler's conservative opponents try to establish contact with the British government. This brought him to the attention of the Gestapo. He was arrested in 1943, imprisoned, and executed in Flossenburg concentration camp in 1945.

SOURCE 3 — Bavarian Catholic bishops' pastoral letter, December 1936

'The Führer can be certain that we bishops are prepared to give all moral support to his historic struggle against communism. We will not criticise things which are purely political.'

The campaign against the Catholics

The Nazis did not stick to their agreement. They were particularly keen to undermine Catholic schools. Instead of banning them, the Nazis interfered with the curriculum, engineered the dismissal of certain teachers and abolished Christian symbols and rituals. There were protests, and in March 1937 the Pope condemned Nazi violations of the Concordat. This did not stop the Nazi campaign. During 1936 and 1937 hundreds of nuns and priests were arrested on charges ranging from illegal currency dealings to child sex abuse.

THE CHURCHES AND NAZI RACIAL POLICIES

Despite this persecution, both Protestants and Catholics were depressingly silent about the Nazis' racial policies. Only a few brave individuals spoke out. One such was Bishop Galen of Münster whose bold sermon in August 1941 caused the suspension, officially at least, of the Nazis' secret campaign of killing Germany's mentally ill patients (see p58).

Questions

1. *Study Source 1. What can you learn from it about the Nazis' attitude to different religions and sects?*
2. *Study Source 2. How useful is it as evidence of Nazi policies towards the Churches?*
3. *Why did the Christian Churches not oppose Nazism more strongly? Explain your answer, using information and sources in this section.*

The persecution of racial enemies and minorities

persecution
systematic or constant cruel treatment of people

The Nazis **persecuted** their racial enemies, especially the Jews, because they believed they had a duty to do so. They maintained that their racial theory provided a scientific explanation of human life. Many thought that Darwin's theory of animal evolution through the 'survival of the fittest' could also be applied to human races. This was called 'Social Darwinism'. It claimed that only the strongest races of humans would survive. The weaker ones would be pushed to the margins of society and eventually die out. Put simply, life was seen as a struggle between 'strong' and 'weak' races to survive.

THE NAZI RACIAL THEORY

- First, Nazis believed that the races of the world were engaged in a life-and-death struggle with one another for survival. The Germans were the 'master-race' whose position was threatened by the inferior races, the worst of whom were the Jews.
- Secondly, Nazis maintained that all human characteristics are inherited. This meant that selective breeding was necessary to ensure the survival of the best and eliminate the weak or undesirable (see Source 1).

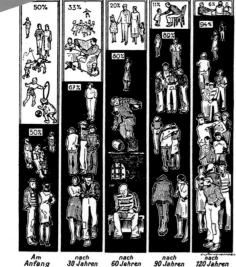

A Nazi chart showing how the German people might become swamped by inferior people unless strong policies were adopted.

- Finally, they argued that the racial community mattered more than individual rights. So, to the Nazis, it was essential to purge Germany, not only of racial enemies such as Jews, but also of criminals, the insane, homosexuals and other 'undesirables'.

NAZI ANTI-SEMITISM IN THE EARLY YEARS, 1933-1934

When Hitler came to power, there were only 500,000 Jews in Germany, less than one per cent of the German population. Hitler had no clear policy towards them. He was more interested in securing his dictatorship. The extremists in the Nazi Party, however, wanted some anti-Jewish measures immediately. Hitler decided on a nationwide boycott of Jewish businesses and professions. He restricted it to a single day to avoid economic disruption. It occurred on April 1, 1933, and reactions were mixed. In some places there was violence but the response of the German public was generally apathetic.

A few days later laws were introduced to evict Jews from the civil service and to restrict their numbers in the legal profession, medicine and schools. President Hindenburg insisted that Jews who had served in the war should be exempt. This meant that 70 per cent of lawyers and 75 per cent of doctors remained in their jobs for the time being.

THE NUREMBERG LAWS, 1935

The Nuremberg Laws, issued on September 15, 1935, were an important milestone in the isolation of Germany's Jews. The Law for the Protection of German Blood and German Honour banned marriages and sex between Germans and Jews. It also prohibited Jews from employing female German servants under 45 years old. The Reich Citizenship Law denied Jews German citizenship. Jews were now officially labelled as second-class citizens.

Further discrimination soon followed. Civil servants spared by the Hindenburg clause were dismissed and Jews were banned from all state service.

SOURCE 2   A sign over a town, reading: 'Jews unwelcome here!'

THE PERSECUTION OF MINORITIES

A law issued on July 14, 1933, required those who were considered to be suffering from mental or hereditary illnesses to be compulsorily sterilised. It is estimated that between 320,000 and 350,000 people were sterilised in accordance with this law.

The mentally ill

euthanasia
normally understood to be the mercy killing of people suffering incurable pain, with the permission of the victim

Hitler was also planning a so-called **euthanasia** programme for the mentally ill. In fact, it was nothing other than murder. According to Nazi theories, caring for such people was a drain on national resources (see Source 4, p53). Furthermore, Hitler believed that allowing them to have children would weaken the German race. In 1938 the Nazis set up a secret committee to organise the killing of deformed babies. Soon after the war started, the programme was extended to adults. Propaganda films were made to convince the German people that this was the right thing to do. By 1941, about 100,000 mentally ill people had been killed.

The 'work-shy', 'asocials' and criminals

asocials
people whose lifestyle or behaviour was different from normal

As the regime grew more powerful it extended the scope of its campaign. There were regular police raids to arrest beggars and vagrants, some of whom were designated 'feeble-minded' and compulsorily sterilised. In April 1938 the Gestapo arrested about 11,000 people for 'anti-social behaviour'. Homosexuals, gypsies and Jehovah's Witnesses became particular targets.

KRISTALLNACHT

On November 7, 1938, a Jewish youth shot and killed a German embassy official in Paris, in revenge for the Nazis' treatment of his parents. Propaganda Minister Josef Goebbels instructed Party members to carry out 'demonstrations' against the Jewish community in Germany during the night of November 9-10. In an orgy of violence, 8,000 Jewish shops and homes were attacked, most synagogues set on fire, about 100 Jews killed and more than 20,000 arrested. There was so much destruction that the event quickly became known as the 'Night of Broken Glass' or *Kristallnacht*. Two days later Goering announced that the Jews were to be fined one billion Reichsmarks for the damage caused on Kristallnacht. A decree was issued formally excluding Jews from economic activity. This allowed Goering to step up the programme of **'Aryanisation'**, by which Jewish property and businesses were bought by Germans at ridiculously low prices.

Aryanisation
process by which the Nazis purged German society of all non-German elements. 'Aryan' describes a white, non-Jewish person

THE SS AND JEWISH EMIGRATION

When Germany took over Austria in March 1938 (see p68), the SS began a ruthless policy of compulsory emigration of Austria's 200,000 Jews. Within six months, a quarter of Austria's Jews had been forced to leave. In February 1939 the policy was extended to the Jews of Germany. But the outbreak of war made emigration difficult. Instead it drove the Nazis into 'the final solution of the Jewish question'.

Questions

1. Study Source 1. What can you learn from it about Nazi ideas about race?
2. Study Source 2. How useful is it as evidence about Nazi policies towards the Jews?
3. 'Nazi racial policies became more extreme from 1938 onwards.' Do you agree with this statement? Explain your answer, using information and sources from this section.

Life in Nazi Germany

SOURCE A   An extract from a Nazi newspaper.

Numerous confessions made by Jews show that devout Jews believe they are required to carry out ritual murder. These murders take place on Jewish religious holy days. They use fresh blood from slaughtered children in their marriage ceremonies. Ritual murder is recognised by all devout Jews. They believe this means that they are forgiven for their sins.

SOURCE B

An SA man guarding a Jewish shop during the Nazi boycott.

SOURCE C   The number of Jews leaving Germany, 1933-39.

Year	Number leaving
1933	37,000
1934	23,000
1935	21,000
1936	25,000
1937	23,000
1938	20,000
1939	78,000

QUESTIONS AND JOHN'S ANSWERS

(a) Study **Source A.**

Do you think this was an effective piece of anti-Jewish propaganda? Use **Source A** and your own knowledge to explain your answer.

(6 marks)

Only about 500,000 Germans were Jewish (less than one per cent of the whole population). Therefore it is likely that most of the German population were very ignorant about Jewish culture and way of life. Most Germans probably only knew about Judaism from what the Nazis told them. However, this source is so exaggerated that most Germans would not take it seriously. But, as part of the Nazis' constant propaganda against the Jews, it probably helped to create negative views about the Jews in the minds of ordinary Germans.

(b) Study **Source B.**

How reliable is this source as evidence that the Nazi boycott of Jewish shops in April 1933 was effective? Use **Source B** and your own knowledge to explain your answer.

(7 marks)

> Source B shows an SA member standing in front of a Jewish shop, encouraging people not to shop there. However, I doubt the reliability of this source as evidence because it may be propaganda. The photograph might have been produced by Goebbels' Propaganda Ministry to convince the German people that the boycott was a success. We know that the boycott passed with little fuss because many Germans did not want to be bullied by the SA. The boycott was also unsuccessful because the Nazi Party originally wanted it to be indefinite, but it was shortened to a single day on Hitler's orders.

(c) Study **Source C.**

Do these statistics suggest that Nazi policy towards Jews was successful? Use **Source C** and your own knowledge to explain your answer.

(7 marks)

> Although 78,000 Jews left Germany in 1939, between 1934 and 1938 relatively few Jews left. Even in 1935, after the introduction of the Nuremberg Laws, still comparatively few Jews left. It was not until the Aryanisation policy and enforced emigration (which started in 1939) that the numbers leaving began to pick up. The number who left in 1939 is high because of the Nazis' radical policy change towards the Jews. Rich Jews were forced to pay for the emigration of poorer ones. Jews were having their property seized by the Nazis and so had few options but to leave. Nazi policy before this (to keep the Jews out of German society) was clearly not as successful as the Nazis had hoped. So they turned to more drastic measures.

HOW TO SCORE FULL MARKS: WHAT THE EXAMINERS SAY

Question (a)

Candidates are required to assess how well a piece of propaganda fulfils its purpose.

This is a good answer. John places the source in its context. But he also shows that, by being so extreme, it was probably not particularly effective. Additionally, he shows that this piece of evidence was part of a relentless campaign to turn the Germans against the Jews, and that this undoubtedly helped to isolate them.

As a result, John received full marks: 6 out of 6.

Question (b)

Candidates are required to comment on the reliability of a source, in relation to a particular issue.

John understands this source well and explains its context effectively. He understands the content of the source but makes intelligent comments about its reliability. He is careful not to dismiss it altogether, but does not accept it at face value as reliable evidence. He uses his knowledge of the boycott skilfully to support his comments on the source.

As a result, John received full marks: 7 out of 7.

Question (c)

Candidates are required to analyse and comment on statistics that relate to a particular issue.

John is correct to show that the Nazi policy towards the Jews had mixed success between 1933 and 1939: the numbers leaving Germany fluctuated. He has a good knowledge of Nazi policies and shows that the Jewish emigration increased as the policy became more severe in 1938 and 1939.

He could have explained why a high number of Jews left in 1933. This was because they feared that the Nazis would immediately start severe persecution. Numbers then dropped because Nazi anti-Semitic policies were relatively mild for a few years.

As a result, John was awarded 5 marks out of a possible 7.

EXTENSION WORK

How much did German society change between 1933 and 1939? Explain your answer, **using sources and information from the last chapter**.

(15 marks)

• AQA accepts no responsibility whatsoever for the accuracy or method of working in the answers given.

Hitler's aims and beliefs

WHAT WAS LEBENSRAUM?

In his book *Mein Kampf* (see p25) Hitler set out the ideas that guided his conduct of foreign policy. He claimed that the Germans were 'the highest species of humanity on this earth'. He also stated that Germany needed to establish an empire in Russia and Eastern Europe because the existing territory of Germany was too small to sustain its growing population. Living space (*lebensraum*) in the east would provide the food and raw materials needed for Germany to establish itself as a world power. He also maintained that Russia had been corrupted by 'Jewish-Communism' and would soon collapse.

SOURCE 1

Hitler's ideas for lebensraum outlined in *Mein Kampf.*

'The acquisition of land and soil is the objective of our foreign policy. We must turn our eyes towards the land in the east – Russia and the states on its borders. Russia's colossal empire is about to collapse because it is dominated by Jews. If we look around for European allies, only two states are possible – England and Italy.'

ADMIRATION FOR BRITAIN

Hitler believed that Britain was Germany's natural ally. He admired the British for ruling a large overseas empire made up of what he saw as inferior Asiatic and African races. His favourite film was *Tales of a Bengal Lancer*, in which a small group of British soldiers heroically defeated an Indian rebellion. He thought that Britain and Germany had a common interest in defeating Russian communism and resisting US power. He believed that Britain should allow Germany to tear up the Treaty of Versailles and become the strongest power in Europe. In return, he would allow Britain to rule its overseas empire in Africa and the Far East without interference from Germany.

THE VERSAILLES SETTLEMENT

Most Germans disliked the Versailles settlement and believed that Germany should be free to fortify the Rhineland and rearm. Hitler's aims went beyond this. He wanted to bring all the German-speaking areas of Europe into his Reich. This would make Germany, not France, the dominant power in Europe. It would also destroy, or turn into German satellites, the countries in Eastern Europe allied to France.

HITLER'S WAR

Hitler loved war and believed that it was natural for men to fight one another. This explains why he called his book 'My Struggle'. He regarded it as his mission in life to win a major war in Eastern Europe to destroy communism and create a German empire that would last 1,000 years. This is why he wanted German mothers to produce more children, especially boys (see p54) and the members of the Hitler Youth to be trained as soldiers (see p52).

But Hitler was also flexible and cunning. He did not reveal his exact plans in advance and was willing to wait for his war until Germany was ready. He was also quite happy to achieve some of his aims peacefully if the western powers, especially Britain, were prepared to give him what he wanted.

HITLER'S POSITION IN 1933

Why did he need to be cautious?

In 1933 Germany was not strong enough economically or militarily to carry out Hitler's ambitious plans. He needed time to establish his dictatorship. Furthermore, Germany had no foreign allies. If Hitler acted too quickly, Britain, France and Italy might join forces to resist him.

What factors encouraged him?
US isolationism

However, the situation in 1933 was potentially favourable. The USA was anxious to stay out of Europe's affairs. Many Americans felt that their soldiers had done enough fighting and dying in

N

LITHUANIA

DENMARK   Baltic Sea

North Sea

EASTERN
PRUSSIA

USSR

German-speaking
peoples, 1919–1939

NETHERLANDS   **G E R M A N Y**

POLAND

BELGIUM

LUXEMBOURG

CZECHOSLOVAKIA

FRANCE

AUSTRIA   HUNGARY

ROMANIA

SWITZERLAND

0   200 km

ITALY   YUGOSLAVIA

the First World War trying to sort out Europe's quarrels. The US Congress even passed laws in 1935 and 1937 to forbid the President from helping any country involved in war. Source 3 shows how little the Americans spent on their armed forces during the 1930s.

European relations

Stalin, in the USSR, wanted to concentrate on building up the Soviet economy and was extremely cautious in his foreign policy. Most European countries feared the USSR more than Germany. Britain and France had disagreed since 1919 about how to treat Germany. The British felt that the Treaty of Versailles had been too harsh and were keen to revise it in Germany's favour. They believed that concessions would make the Germans more co-operative. The French wanted to enforce the Treaty but could not do so properly without full British support. They had learnt their lesson from the failure of their invasion of the Ruhr in 1923 (see p20).

Effects of the Depression

Finally, the Depression had made it more difficult for democratic governments to find the money for armaments. This was shown by their reluctance to respond strongly when the Japanese invaded the Chinese province of

Manchuria in 1931. For most of the 1930s, Britain lagged behind Germany in its military spending (see Source 3).

SOURCE 3	Percentage of national wealth devoted to armaments, 1929-1939.		
YEAR	GERMANY	BRITAIN	USA
1929	1%	2%	1%
1933	3%	3%	1%
1936	13%	5%	1%
1938	17%	8%	1%
1939	23%	22%	1%

Questions

1. Study Source 2.
   a) How does it help you to understand why the British were sympathetic to Hitler when he said he wanted to change the Treaty of Versailles?
   b) How does it help you to understand why the French were reluctant to allow Hitler to change the Treaty of Versailles?
2. Why do you think Hitler wanted to have Britain as an ally? Explain your answer, using information and sources from this section.

The economy under the Nazis

HITLER'S ECONOMIC AIMS

When Hitler came to power his main economic aim was to prepare Germany for war. He believed this involved more than just building up the strength of the armed forces. He was obsessed by Germany's defeat in 1918 and attributed it to the collapse of morale on the home front. So, as well as preparing people for war with education and propaganda, he aimed to keep the population happy by maintaining high living standards. He also wanted to reduce the amount that Germany needed to import from abroad. This would make a British naval blockade of German ports less effective.

HITLER'S IMMEDIATE PRIORITIES

Getting people back to work
Promising to end Germany's political and economic weakness had made the Nazis popular, so Hitler had to get the German people back to work as quickly as possible. The government immediately began a programme of building canals, roads, bridges, houses and public buildings. They also put money into the railways and developed land improvement schemes. Unemployment fell rapidly, from six million in January 1933, to 300,000 in January 1939.

ideology
a set of ideas or beliefs held by a particular group of people

Agriculture
Because farmers worked on the soil of Germany, they had a special place in Nazi ideology. Farmers had also helped the Nazis into power by voting for them in large numbers. This is why Hitler placed agriculture alongside unemployment as the first two economic problems to be solved in 1933. Unfortunately, Nazi policies only worsened the situation. Young men left the countryside in large numbers to get jobs in the construction projects that the Nazis had begun. Farmers bitterly resented having to sell their produce at government-controlled prices to the Nazis' marketing organisation – the Reich Food Estate. Although in 1934 the government launched a drive to increase production, Germany soon faced a shortage of home-produced animal meat and dairy products.

Rearmament
The Nazis also began a programme of rearmament. They were helped by the president of the Reichsbank, Hjalmar Schacht. He invented a clever accounting system to keep the rearmament secret from foreign observers. In 1934 Hitler made him Minister of Economics, as well.

SOURCE 1 — An SPD agent reports on discontent among the peasants in 1934.

'The peasants of Oldenburg and East Friesland, who were once enthusiastic Nazis, are now rejecting the Party. It is controls on the sale of milk and eggs that are responsible. The farms near towns previously delivered their milk direct to the consumer and received 16 pfennigs per litre. Now the consumer pays 20 pfennigs per litre, but the farmer receives only 10-12 pfennigs.'

HOW DID HITLER DEAL WITH THE CRISIS OF 1936?

By 1936 an economic crisis was looming. Germany could not import increasing quantities of raw materials for her construction boom and simultaneously buy more food from abroad. Hitler was faced with an unpleasant choice. He did not wish to risk unpopularity by imposing food rationing. Nor did he want to cut spending on rearmament.

The Four Year Plan, 1936-1940
His solution was to launch a Four Year Plan under the leadership of Goering. This aimed to make the country completely self-sufficient. Massive investment was put into making Germany a leading world producer of iron and steel using her own resources of iron-ore, even though these were more expensive and of inferior quality to the ore available from Sweden. Furthermore, big contracts were given to a chemical firm called IG Farben to produce synthetic rubber and to extract oil from coal and coke. In his secret memorandum setting up the Plan, Hitler declared that he wanted the

SOURCE 2 — Hitler's Economic Memorandum that created the Four Year Plan, 1936.

'Apart from Germany and Italy, only Japan can be considered as a power standing firm in the face of the world peril posed by communism. A victory of communism over Germany would lead to the annihilation of the German people. If we do not succeed in bringing the German army as rapidly as possible to the rank of premier army in the world, then Germany will be lost. Now, with iron determination, a 100 per cent self-sufficiency should be achieved in every sphere where it is possible. I thus set the following tasks:

1. The German armed forces must be operational within four years.
2. The German economy must be fit for war within four years.'

How far had the Nazis achieved their economic goals by 1939?

The army
The German armed forces were a great deal stronger than they had been in 1933 and were well equipped to fight a series of short **blitzkrieg** wars. But the economy was not fully geared for war in the way that Hitler had intended. Nor was it self-sufficient.

blitzkrieg
lightning war: a rapid campaign to destroy the enemy's armed forces in a few weeks

Unemployment
Unemployment had been eliminated and there was even a shortage of skilled labour by 1939. Many Germans felt grateful to Hitler for restoring prosperity. But not everyone's living standard improved. Many workers were on low-paid or part-time jobs. Rearmament was paid for by higher taxes. The consumption of beer – always a good measure of people's prosperity – actually went down during the Third Reich.

Agriculture
The Nazis certainly did not solve the problems of German agriculture. 1.5 million workers left the countryside between 1933 and 1939 and, although the Nazis had some success in boosting arable production, they did not succeed in making German agriculture self-sufficient.

SOURCE 3 — The aims and achievements of the Four Year Plan (in thousands of tons).

Commodity per year	Plan target	1936 output	1938 output	1942 output
Oil/synthetic petrol	13,830	1,790	2,340	6,260
Synthetic rubber	120	0.7	5	96
Explosives	223	18	45	300
Iron ore	5,549	2,255	3,360	4,137
Hard coal	213,000	158,400	186,186	166,059

German economy and armed forces ready for war within four years.

In 1937 Schacht resigned in disgust. He thought the Four Year Plan was foolishly uneconomic. He was correct, but this did not matter to the Nazis. The production of war materials expanded rapidly. By 1939, 65 per cent of investment was going into war-related industries. Even though the targets for synthetic production were not met and German heavy industry remained dependent on Swedish iron-ore, there were huge increases in output.

Questions

1. Study Source 1. How does it help you to understand why Nazi agricultural policies were not successful?
3. Study Source 2. What can you learn from it about Hitler's economic aims?
4. Study Source 3. Which parts of the Four Year Plan were most successful? Which were least successful? Explain your answer.

Hitler's foreign policy, 1933-37

WHAT WERE HITLER'S FIRST MOVES?

When Hitler came to power, the European nations had been meeting in Geneva since 1932 to try to agree about reducing the size of their armed forces. Hitler was not interested in this. He withdrew Germany from both the disarmament talks and the League of Nations in October 1933. He skilfully blamed the French for his decision by pointing out that they did not want Germany's armed forces to be as powerful as theirs. Hitler then made his first move to undermine the French alliance system in Eastern Europe by signing a ten-year non-aggression pact with Poland in January 1934.

THE ATTEMPTED ANSCHLUSS, 1934

Anschluss
the union of Germany and Austria to create a single German state

An opportunity to unite Germany with Hitler's homeland, Austria, presented itself in the summer of 1934. Some Nazis, probably acting on their own initiative, murdered the Austrian Chancellor and invited Hitler to invade and restore order. But the Italian dictator, Mussolini, made it clear that he would resist a German invasion of Austria. Hitler decided to do nothing because he knew that he was not yet ready for war.

GERMAN REARMAMENT

By March 1935 Hitler was ready to test European reactions to his rearmament programme. He announced that Germany was building an air force and that the German army would soon be 550,000 strong. The British, French and Italians met in April to denounce these violations of the Versailles Treaty but the solidarity of this trio was quickly undermined by the British government. By the terms of the Anglo-German Naval Agreement signed in June, Germany was permitted to build a fleet a third the size of the British navy. There were to be no restrictions on **U-boats**. Hitler actually had no plans to rebuild his fleet at this time but the agreement showed him clearly that Britain would not resist his plans to tear up the disarmament clauses of the Versailles Treaty.

U-boats
German submarines

SOURCE 1

The swearing-in of new recruits to Germany's expanded army, 1935.

ABYSSINIA, OCTOBER 1935

Hitler was even more delighted when Mussolini invaded the African state of Abyssinia (now called Ethiopia) in October 1935. There had been every chance that the Italians might interfere in his plans for Central Europe; now their attention was drawn elsewhere. Furthermore, Britain and France felt bound to condemn Mussolini's action. This made a European coalition of Britain, France and Italy against Germany even less likely.

THE RHINELAND, MARCH 1936

With the European powers distracted by the Abyssinian crisis, Hitler decided to send German troops into the demilitarised Rhineland. He knew he was taking a risk. The Rhineland had been demilitarised in 1919 to prevent any future German invasion of France (see p19). If the French failed to react it would be a clear sign that they lacked the will to resist his plans. To seduce the British, Hitler emphasised his peaceful intentions, promised to consider re-joining the League of Nations and offered to sign a non-aggression pact.

SOURCE 2

German troops enter the Rhineland, March 1936

The British had no intention of reacting to his action. Their pressure prevented the French from doing anything either. Hitler's prestige in Germany soared. He had, in effect, torn up the hated Treaty of Versailles without firing a shot.

THE SPANISH CIVIL WAR, 1936-1939

Hitler's room for manoeuvre was further widened by the outbreak of civil war in Spain. With Stalin offering tentative help to one side, Mussolini providing considerable aid to the other, and Britain and France staying nervously neutral, the attention of Europe was nicely distracted. Hitler was even able to test his new air force in a devastating raid on the Basque town of Guernica. However, he resisted getting fully involved because he wanted the war to go on as long as possible.

HITLER TAKES THE INITIATIVE

By November 1937 Hitler felt ready to act decisively. He held a secret conference with his top military advisers and told them that he intended to take over Austria and Czechoslovakia in the near future. He said that Britain, although it now had to be considered an enemy, was unlikely to object. Three of the men present expressed concern about the risks involved in these plans, and Hitler sacked them a few months later. They were replaced by men who either supported his aggressive intentions, or did not dare to criticise him.

> **! INVESTIGATE...**
> Build your own timeline of key events in Nazi foreign policy, 1933-1937. Go to www.spartacus.schoolnet.co.uk/ GERnazigermany.htm

Questions

1. In what ways did the other countries of Europe help Hitler to achieve his aims in the 1930s? Make a list, using information and sources from this section.
2. Why did Hitler decide to become more aggressive in the autumn of 1937? Explain your answer, using information and sources from this section and elsewhere in this book.

The road to war, 1938-39

Hitler had clear ideas about his foreign policy aims, but he was not working to a timetable. His actions in 1938 and 1939 demonstrate that his policy was a mixture of ruthlessness, improvisation and flexibility.

THE ANSCHLUSS WITH AUSTRIA

Although he had not been able to take over Austria in 1934, Hitler had always planned to incorporate the country of his birth into Germany as part of his drive to unite all German-speaking people in his Reich. He knew that Britain would not object and that, without British support, the French would be unable to resist. By 1938 Mussolini was an ally and could be persuaded to accept it. When the Austrian chancellor, Kurt von Schuschnigg, decided to hold a plebiscite about Austria's future, Hitler was forced to act. He could not risk the Austrians voting to reject union with Germany. On March 12, 1938, the German army crossed the frontier. It met no resistance, but the invasion had been organised so hastily that one tank unit had to use a tourist map and refuel at roadside petrol stations. On March 15, Hitler himself proclaimed the union of the two countries in a triumphal speech to the crowds in Vienna.

plebiscite
a vote by the people on a single issue

THE CRISIS OVER THE SUDETENLAND

Hitler now planned to destroy Czechoslovakia. However, he was not yet ready for a major war. He also knew that Czechoslovakia had an alliance with France and the USSR. Hitler decided to use the grievances of the three million Germans who lived in Czechoslovakia's frontier region – the Sudetenland – to create a crisis. He instructed the leader of the Sudeten Germans to make trouble for the Czech government. Hitler hoped that, if he could portray the Czechs as oppressors of a German minority, the European powers would refuse to support Czechoslovakia when Germany invaded.

CHAMBERLAIN'S APPEASEMENT

However, Hitler's plans were obstructed by the British Prime Minister, Neville Chamberlain, who was determined to find a peaceful solution to the crisis. Chamberlain made the mistake of thinking that Hitler only wanted to unite the Sudeten Germans with the Reich. He visited Germany three times and worked hard to persuade the French and Czechs to accept the transfer of the Sudetenland to Germany. At the third meeting, held in Munich at the end of September 1938, Hitler reluctantly accepted Chamberlain's plan. He realised that Britain and France were prepared to declare war if he used force. As he remarked to an aide, "That damned fellow Chamberlain has spoilt my entry into Prague." Chamberlain's policy was known as 'Appeasement'.

SOURCE 1 Hitler and Chamberlain at their first meeting in September 1938.

THE DESTRUCTION OF CZECHOSLOVAKIA

Within a month of the Munich agreement, Hitler had ordered his generals to prepare for 'the liquidation of the remainder of the Czech state'. His orders were carried out on 15 March, 1939, when German troops entered Prague. This action shocked opinion worldwide because it could not be justified as merely uniting German-speakers. Prague was not part of the Sudetenland. Britain and France did nothing, but made a public pledge to defend the independence of Hitler's next potential victim – Poland.

German expansion during the 1930s.

- - - Germany's border in 1933
- Extent of Germany's expansion by July 1939

N

DENMARK

LITHUANIA
MEMEL

North Sea

EASTERN PRUSSIA

RHINELAND, remilitarised by Hitler in 1936

Berlin

Warsaw

P O L A N D

G E R M A N Y

SUDETENLAND

Prague

C Z E C H O S L O V A K I A

SAAR, regained in 1935

FRANCE

Vienna

Budapest

A U S T R I A

H U N G A R Y

SWITZERLAND

ITALY

0   200 km

SOURCE 3

Hitler's foreign ministers with Stalin and his foreign minister, Molotov, after signing the Nazi-Soviet Pact, August 1939.

SOURCE 4

Hitler explains his plans to a foreign diplomat in August 1939.

"Everything I undertake is directed against the Soviets. If the West is too stupid and blind to grasp this, I shall be compelled to come to an agreement with the Soviets, beat the West, and then, after their defeat, turn against the Soviet Union with all my forces."

THE ROLE OF THE USSR

Both Hitler and the Western Allies realised that this pledge was worthless unless the USSR could be persuaded to assist Poland. This was because the USSR was the only major power which could bring troops to Poland's assistance quick enough. But the efforts of Britain and France to secure Soviet help were unsuccessful. Stalin, after the Munich agreement, was extremely suspicious of their motives and feared they wanted to leave all the fighting to his Red Army. Furthermore, the Poles did not want to be helped by the USSR and refused to allow Soviet troops onto their soil. This made possible Hitler's most surprising, and cynical, move.

THE NAZI-SOVIET PACT, AUGUST 1939

At the end of August 1939 Hitler's foreign minister flew to Moscow and rapidly agreed a deal with Stalin. Germany and the USSR signed a ten-year Non-Aggression Pact. In a secret clause they also divided Poland between them and carved up Eastern Europe into 'spheres of influence'.

The Pact left Poland defenceless, and the Second World War began when Germany attacked on September 1. Two days later Britain and France declared war on Germany.

SOURCE 5

The British Foreign Secretary explains his country's tougher attitude to Germany after Hitler's invasion of Poland, June 29, 1939.

'In the past we have always stood out against any single power attempting to dominate Europe at the expense of the liberties of other nations. We know that, if the security and independence of other countries are to disappear, our own security and our own independence will be gravely threatened. We know that if international law and order is to be preserved, we must be prepared to fight in its defence.'

Questions

1. Study Source 2. Compare it with Source 2 on p63. Which territories that Hitler gained between 1933 and 1937 could be justified and explained as part of his plan to unite German-speaking people? Explain your answer.
2. Study Source 5. Why did the British government adopt a tougher approach to Germany in 1939?
3. At what point do you think Britain and France could, and should, have stopped Hitler's expansion? Explain your answer, using information and sources in this section.

Preparing for war

SOURCE A

A report by the German army's economic experts in Munich, September 1938.

The theatres are fully booked, the cinemas are full and the cafés are overflowing into the early hours with music and dancing. And yet, despite all these signs of a favourable economic situation, large numbers of people are depressed about the future. They fear that a war will sooner or later put an end to the economic revival and have terrible consequences for Germany.

SOURCE B

From a letter to Hitler from a member of his government, October 1936.

As a result of the strong revival in the German economy, a severe shortage of skilled workers has developed in the building trade, in the building materials industry and in the metal industry. 50,000 more metal workers will shortly be needed for the new aircraft factories. Many employers have been poaching skilled workers from other factories by offering excessively high wages. The size of their wage increases is sometimes as high as three times the normal rate.

SOURCE C

German Labour Front poster.

Deutsche Arbeitsfront

SOURCE D

From a report by the Gestapo in Düsseldorf, 1937.

After factory meetings at which speakers of the Labour Front had spoken, some of whom were in fact rather clumsy in their statements, the mood of discontent among the workers was apparent in subsequent discussions. In one fairly large factory, the speaker from the Labour Front greeted the workers with the Hitler salute, but in reply the workers only mumbled. When the speaker ended the meeting with another Hitler salute, the workers replied loudly and clearly, but only because the meeting had come to an end.

QUESTIONS AND STEPHEN'S ANSWER

(a) Compare **Source A** and **Source B**. Do they agree about the success of Nazi economic policies between 1933 and 1939?

(6 marks)

> These two sources do agree about the success of Nazi economic policies between 1933 and 1939. They both show that the Nazis were successful. Source A talks about a favourable economic situation and Source B says that there was a strong revival of the German economy. However, Source B says that problems were developing by 1936.

(b) How reliable is **Source B** as evidence about the economy in Nazi Germany?

(9 marks)

> This source is very reliable. It was written by a member of Hitler's government, who would have preferred to tell Hitler good news. Since he is telling him bad news, he is probably telling the truth. I know that the Nazi policies of building and rearming were causing shortages, so this is a reliable source.

(c) Sources **C** and **D** give different views about the attitude of workers to the Nazis. In what ways do they differ? Use **Sources C** and **D** and your own knowledge to explain your answer.

(10 marks)

These two sources come from different points of view. Source C is an image provided by the German Labour Front and shows how the Nazis wanted the German people to be. It shows a worker, building a wall, with active factories and a large Nazi swastika in th background. It is a

propaganda poster that suggests the Nazis and the DAF are working together to build Germany's future. The factories in the background represent Hitler's war production drive. In contrast, Source D shows that there was not actually the unity that the Nazis aimed for. It shows a mood of discontent among the workers. The sources show that there was a big difference between the aims of the Nazis and what actually happened. But both sources are from the Nazis. Source C is propaganda, so it is not really reliable, but there was no reason for the Gestapo to tell lies, so Source D is reliable.

HOW TO SCORE FULL MARKS: WHAT THE EXAMINERS SAY

Question (a)
Candidates are required to compare and contrast two sources relating to one issue, and decide how they are similar and how they differ.

Stephen makes some excellent points of comparison and shows that both sources refer to the economic successes achieved by the Nazis. However, Stephen could have developed his points about the problems that both sources refer to. Source A points out that the German people's fears about the future might cause economic problems. Source B indicates that the severe problems of inflation, the shortage of skilled workers, and the poaching of workers were the product of the Nazis' own policies.

As a result, Stephen received 3 out a possible 6 marks.

Question (b)
Candidates are required to assess the reliability of a source, in relation to a particular issue.

Stephen has written a good answer. He assesses both the provenance of the source (who wrote it and why), as well as its content. He correctly concludes that it is a reliable source. However, he could have pointed out that we have no way of knowing whether Hitler actually read the letter or whether it influenced his decisions. The source is also very specific about the problems the German economy faced in 1936, which makes it useful, as well as reliable.

As a result, Stephen received 7 out of a possible 9 marks.

Question (c)
Candidates are required to compare and contrast two sources relating to one issue, and use their own knowledge to point out the similarities and differences between them.

Stephen analyses the sources skilfully, but does not support his ideas with any knowledge of his own. He explains that Source C was a propaganda image showing what the Nazis wanted and contrasts this with Source D, which reveals that some workers did not support the Nazis. He makes good comments on the reliability of the sources. However, he needs to use his own knowledge to explain why the Nazis did not devote as much attention to winning working-class support as they did to other policies and why some workers failed to be won over.

As a result, Stephen was awarded 7 out of a possible 10 marks.

EXTENSION WORK

How well had Hitler prepared Germany and its people for the outbreak of war in 1939? Explain your answer, **using sources and information in the last chapter.**

(15 marks)

• AQA accepts no responsibility whatsoever for the accuracy or method of working in the anwers given.

Everyday life in wartime Germany

ATTITUDES TO THE WAR

Early support

In some ways the loyalty of the German people to the Nazi regime increased during the war. Hitler was at the height of his popularity in 1940 when his stunning victory over France appeared to have brought a swift and successful end to the war. Most Germans were patriotic and supported the war effort, particularly when Germany became subject to intense Allied terror bombing from 1943 onwards (see Source 3).

Growing doubts

Serious doubts about the war grew once the Germans started to lose. In contravention of the Nazi-Soviet pact, Germany invaded the USSR in 1941, with initial success. But Hitler's popularity dwindled after the defeat by Soviet forces at Stalingrad in January 1943. He was widely seen as personally responsible for this disaster because he had refused to let the German army withdraw from the city. Stalingrad was the turning point of the war on the eastern front and meant that the Germans were on the defensive as the Soviets slowly and surely pushed them back. However, fear of being conquered by the communist USSR made many Germans grimly loyal to the Nazis as the lesser of two evils.

CONDITIONS IN WARTIME

As in all the countries involved, life in Germany became tougher for ordinary citizens. Everyday goods like food, fuel and clothes were expensive because they were in short supply. Most basic foods were rationed as soon as the war started. German citizens were also much more likely to suffer from bombing than people in Britain. Over 300,000 Germans died and 780,000 were injured as a result of allied bombs. This compares with 60,000 Britons killed by German bombs.

SOURCE 2

Adult rations for a four-week period (in grams).

Date	Meat	Fat	Bread	Sugar	Cheese
Oct 1939	2000	1080	9600	1160	250
May 1941	2000	1077.5	9000	1350	250
Jan 1943	1600	825	9000	1250	125
June 1944	1200	875	10900	1250	187.5
April 1945	550	300	3600	375	62.5

SOURCE 1

A Gestapo report on morale in Germany in July 1943.

'The telling of vulgar jokes critical of the state, even about the Führer himself, has increased considerably since Stalingrad. They clearly assume that any joke can now be told without fear of being reported to the police. Large sections of the population, and even a section of the Party membership, have clearly lost the feeling that listening to, and passing on, political jokes is something which a decent German simply does not do.'

SOURCE 3

Dresden after Allied bombing in February 1945.

Two men cut up a dead horse for meat at a German roadside, 1945.

SOURCE 4

CONSCRIPTION

German men had been made liable for military service as early as 1935 when Hitler reintroduced **conscription**, in defiance of the Treaty of Versailles. The Nazis were reluctant to conscript women for war work because they believed that women should stay at home. Even so, women workers were essential. A third of the German workforce was female in 1939 and, in 1943, all women between the ages of 17 and 45 became liable for war work.

conscription
compulsory service in the armed forces or war production factories

This did not solve Germany's acute labour shortage, which the Nazis tried to solve by turning prisoners of war into slave labourers. By the end of the war, there were over seven million foreign workers in Germany.

MANAGING THE ECONOMY

The Nazis did not run their economy efficiently during the war. This was because too many individuals and organisations were battling with one another for control. In February 1942 Hitler made Albert Speer his Minister of Armaments and gave him the power to control the economy. Speer introduced mass production techniques and managed to increase the output of armaments from German factories, despite the disruption caused by Allied bombing. But this was never going to be enough to challenge the industrial might of the USSR and the USA.

REPRESSION

During the war, the Nazis became even more determined to prevent opposition. New laws to restrict behaviour were passed. Even listening to foreign radio broadcasts could be punished by the death penalty. The number of people detained in concentration camps increased dramatically (see Source 5), although many of

these were foreigners. Special courts were established to deal with wartime offenders and there was a steep rise in the number of executions. In 1942, the SS decided that long-term prisoners and racial enemies in the camps should be 'worked to death'. Nevertheless, the Nazis were anxious to maintain civilian morale during the war, which meant that ordinary Germans did not really face additional terror. It was the groups that the Nazis already regarded as enemies who suffered most.

SOURCE 5	Concentration camp inmates.
September 1939	25,000
December 1942	88,000
January 1945	714,000

Questions

1. *Study Source 1. How reliable is it as evidence of Germans' opinion of the Nazi regime during the war? Explain your answer.*
2. *Study Source 2. Plot the rations on a graph using different colours for each commodity. What conclusions can you draw from your graph about when conditions became seriously bad for the German people?*
3. *Study Source 4. How useful is it as evidence about German morale during the war?*
4. *'Ordinary Germans lost their faith in Hitler and the Nazis after the defeat at Stalingrad.' Do you agree with this statement? Explain your answer, using information and sources in this section.*

Who resisted Hitler?

ARMY OPPOSITION

Most army officers were delighted with Hitler's policies. They shared his hatred of the Treaty of Versailles and the Weimar Republic, and welcomed the speed with which he rebuilt the armed forces and restored Germany's international prestige. A few of them despised Nazi vulgarity and looked down on the humble social origins of the Party leadership. But they were reassured when the Night of the Long Knives (see p43) ended Ernst Roehm's ambitions to become Commander-in-Chief of the army.

Beck's conspiracy, 1938

A small group of officers led by General Beck, the Chief of the General Staff, developed doubts in 1938. They thought Hitler's conduct of the Czech crisis was recklessly risking a war with Britain and France that Germany could not win. However, the Munich agreement (see p68), which seemed to be another bloodless triumph for Hitler, ended their hopes of a coup.

ATTEMPTS TO ASSASSINATE HITLER

There was no whisper of opposition within the army during the period of Hitler's spectacular victories between 1939 and 1942. But the grumbles returned after the shattering German defeat at Stalingrad in January 1943. This failure was widely attributed to Hitler himself. The defeat also put the Germans permanently on the defensive in the east and made it clear that Germany would ultimately lose the war (see p72). Fear of defeat by the USSR and the idea of communist rule appalled many Germans.

During 1942 Hans Oster, a colonel in army intelligence, gathered together a group of conservatives who disliked Nazi policies and felt that Hitler was leading Germany to disaster. They concluded that the assassination of Hitler was essential. Several attempts in 1943 to kill him failed, mostly because of bad luck and Hitler's habit of changing his plans at the last minute.

THE JULY BOMB PLOT, 1944

Germany's deteriorating military position in 1944 prompted the most famous attempt on Hitler's life. Klaus von Stauffenberg, whose rank and position enabled him to attend Hitler's conferences, planned to leave a bomb in the Führer's eastern HQ. After Hitler's death, the Home Army would seize Berlin and arrest the major Nazi leaders and set up a new government headed by Beck. The conspirators felt they had to act quickly to try to secure a negotiated peace with the Allies.

| SOURCE 1 | Stauffenberg, on the left, meeting Hitler. This photograph was taken five days before the unsuccessful assassination attempt. |

The plot fails

On July 20, 1944, Stauffenberg succeeded in planting his bomb inside a briefcase in Hitler's HQ, and then left. Unfortunately, someone moved the briefcase, so that when the bomb exploded Hitler escaped with only slight injuries. In Berlin, caution and uncertainty prevented the conspirators from acting decisively. General Fromm, whom Stauffenberg had hoped would lead the Home Army in the coup, arrested the conspirators and had them shot.

| SOURCE 2 | Hitler's reaction to the attempt on his life. |

"I will put their wives and children into concentration camps and show them no mercy."

Goering inspects the damage to Hitler's HQ made by Stauffenberg's bomb.

Hitler's revenge

The tragedy of Stauffenberg's courageous attempt was that it never had much chance of success. The conspirators lacked popular support in Germany, and the Allies had already made it clear that they would accept nothing but unconditional surrender. Hitler took terrible revenge on anyone associated with the conspirators. About 200 were tried and hanged. Their executions were filmed, so that Hitler could watch them. But, as one conspirator remarked before he died, an attempt to kill Hitler had to be made, if only to show that not all Germans were Nazis.

> **SOURCE 4**   Sophie Scholl's statement at her trial.
>
> *"What we said and wrote is what many people are thinking. Only they don't dare say it."*

Parties and individuals

These army officers were not the only Germans to oppose the Nazis. Communists and Socialists, although they were subject to close surveillance by the Gestapo, kept their resistance alive by holding secret meetings, distributing leaflets and supporting one another in times of difficulty. Their resistance never threatened the regime, but they did not allow themselves to become part of the Nazis' national community.

Courageous individuals also voiced their opposition and many suffered the consequences. Some were Christians like Dietrich Bonhoeffer (see p57) and others acted out of conscience. A remarkable brother and sister, Hans and Sophie Scholl (see Sources 4 and 5), protested about Nazi barbarities and distributed leaflets among their fellow students at Munich University. They were executed in February 1943.

SOURCE 5

Hans and Sophie Scholl.

Questions

1. *Why do you think there wasn't more support from within the German army for Stauffenberg's plot?*
2. *Write the diary entry that Stauffenberg might have composed the night before he planted his bomb. How might he have justified his action?*
3. *Study Source 4. Do you think Sophie Scholl was correct in what she said at her trial? Explain your answer.*
4. *Make a list of the different groups and individuals who disliked the Nazis. Why do you think they were unable to work together?*

Racial cleansing and the Holocaust

HIMMLER'S RACIAL PLANS FOR POLAND

On October 7, 1939, within days of the conquest of Poland, Himmler was given the job of implementing the Nazis' ambitious racial schemes for that country. The territories lost at Versailles became part of the Reich. All German territory was now called 'Greater Germany'. Ethnic Poles and Poland's three million Jews were to be expelled to the central area of Poland, which the Nazis called the General Government. Germans from the Baltic republics, like Lithuania, were to be moved in. It is unlikely that there were any plans for the mass murder of the Jews at this stage. Indeed, Himmler appears to have given priority to the re-settlement of Germans. Within the Reich itself, German Jews were still being encouraged to emigrate.

An Einsatzgruppen execution of a Polish Jew, in Poland.

THE GHETTOS

The Polish Jews were rounded up and forced into the major cities to live in over crowded slums, called ghettos. Meanwhile, the Nazi leaders argued amongst themselves about their fate. There was even a suggestion in the summer of 1940 that the Jews should be shipped *en masse* to the French colony of Madagascar. Hans Frank, the Nazi in charge of the General Government, tried, unsuccessfully, to resist Himmler's plan to move millions of Jews into his area.

THE INVASION OF THE USSR, 1941

The situation was transformed by the German invasion of the USSR in June 1941, which made the war into a crusade to destroy communism. Hitler told his generals that this was to be a war of extermination, and instructed them to show no mercy to the people they conquered in the east. Furthermore, there were another five million Jews living in the USSR.

Einsatzgruppen
Behind the lines of advancing troops, the SS sent in units called 'special task squads' (*Einsatzgruppen*) whose job was to murder anyone able to organise resistance. Inevitably, their victims included a large number of Jews.

THE DECISION TO BEGIN THE HOLOCAUST

It is impossible to ascertain exactly when the Nazis decided on the mass killing of the Jews. There are no clear written orders from Hitler, although it is inconceivable that such a major decision could have been taken without his knowledge. He created a climate in which extreme measures could be adopted when, in January 1939, he declared that, if war came, it would result in the "annihilation" of the Jews.

SOURCE 2

Hitler threatens the Jews with annihilation in a speech to the Reichstag in January 1939.

"If the international Jewish financiers in and outside Europe should succeed in plunging the nations once more into a world war, then it will not result in the world becoming communist and thus giving the Jews a victory, but in the annihilation of the Jewish race in Europe."

By the summer of 1941 a number of pressures to find a solution came together. Himmler wanted to find a 'humane' way of carrying out executions because his Einsatzgruppen were finding the mass shootings a strain. By December they were using the gas vans first

Nazi death camps and concentration camps within 'Greater Germany'.

The incinerators at Majdanek, used to burn the bodies of murdered Jews.

employed in the euthanasia campaign against the mentally ill. In October 1941 the Nazis began transporting German Jews to the already overcrowded ghettos of Poland. This forced the Nazi authorities there to find a rapid and so-called 'final solution to the Jewish problem'.

THE DEATH CAMPS

The first extermination camp was opened at Chelmno in December 1941. During 1942 the purpose-built death camps at Belzec, Sobibor, Auschwitz, Treblinka and Majdanek were established (see Source 5). The Jews of Eastern Europe were transported from the Polish ghettos and murdered in their millions at these factories of death.

Himmler justifies the Holocaust to his SS leaders in October 1943.

"We had the moral right, we had the duty to our people, to destroy this people which wanted to destroy us. We have exterminated a bacterium because we do not want, in the end, to be infected by the bacterium and die of it."

THE HOLOCAUST IN EUROPE

The Nazis also cast their net much wider. At a conference held in a villa in Wannsee, a smart suburb of Berlin, in January 1942, the SS drew up plans to kill all the Jews of Europe. In all the countries under German rule or influence, Jews were systematically rounded up and transported to the east. By November 1944, when gassing ceased at Auschwitz – the last camp to close – approximately 5.7 million Jews had been killed. This was 68 per cent of the pre-war Jewish population of the conquered territories. This terrible destruction of the European Jews became known as the Holocaust.

Questions

1. Study Sources 1, 3 and 5. Why did the murder of the Jews change from a series of executions (Source 1) to a systematic campaign organised like an industry (Sources 3 and 5)?
2. Study Sources 2 and 4.
   a) How useful are they as evidence about why the Nazis carried out the Holocaust?
   b) How does Source 4 help you to understand why the Nazis attempted to murder all the Jews of Europe?
3. Why did the Holocaust happen at the same time as the war in the USSR? Explain your answer using information and sources from this section.

Every effort has been made to contact the holders of copyright material, but if any have been inadvertently overlooked the publishers will be pleased to make the necessary arrangements at the first opportunity.

The author and publishers gratefully acknowledge the use of examination questions from the awarding body Edexcel 48,49.

The publishers would like to thank the following for permission to reproduce pictures on these pages.

(T=Top, B=Bottom, L=Left, R=Right, C=Centre)

AKG-London 15, 21, 26cl, 29, 32, 42, 45b, 47bl, 47cr, 48, 50tl, 51, Kahlenberger Bauernfamilie, by Adolf Wissell 1939 55, 57, 66, 70, 74, 75t,bl,br; The Art Archive/Imperial War Museum 47br; Corbis/©Bettmann 35, Corbis/©Hulton-Deutsch Collection 10, 13, 33; Popperfoto 8, 14, 22, 25, 26br, 28, 34, 40, 44, 46b, 52bl, 67, 69, 72, 76; Robert Hunt Library 11, 16, 24, 30, 31, 43, 46t, 50b, 52tr, 59, 60, 68, 73, 77.

Cover picture: portrait of Adolf Hitler from Signal magazine, 1941. The Bridgeman Art Library.

Index